C000126494

Request For Information
Complete Self-Assessment Guide

The guidance in this Self-Assessment is based on Request For Information best practices and standards in business process architecture, design and quality management. The guidance is also based on the professional judgment of the individual collaborators listed in the Acknowledgments.

Notice of rights

Trademarks

Table of Contents

About The Art of Service

The Art of Service, Business Process Architects since 2000, is dedicated to helping stakeholders achieve excellence.

Defining, designing, creating, and implementing a process to solve a stakeholders challenge or meet an objective is the most valuable role... In EVERY group, company, organization and department.

Unless you're talking a one-time, single-use project, there should be a process. Whether that process is managed and implemented by humans, AI, or a combination of the two, it needs to be designed by someone with a complex enough perspective to ask the right questions.

Someone capable of asking the right questions and step back and say, 'What are we really trying to accomplish here? And is there a different way to look at it?'

With The Art of Service's Standard Requirements Self-Assessments, we empower people who can do just that — whether their title is marketer, entrepreneur, manager, salesperson, consultant, Business Process Manager, executive assistant, IT Manager, CIO etc... —they are the people who rule the future. They are people who watch the process as it happens, and ask the right questions to make the process work better.

Contact us when you need any support with this Self-Assessment and any help with templates, blue-prints and examples of standard documents you might need:

http://theartofservice.com
service@theartofservice.com

Included Resources - how to access

Included with your purchase of the book is the Request For

Information Self-Assessment Spreadsheet Dashboard which contains all questions and Self-Assessment areas and auto-generates insights, graphs, and project RACI planning - all with examples to get you started right away.

How? Simply send an email to
access@theartofservice.com
with this books' title in the subject to get the Request For Information Self Assessment Tool right away.

You will receive the following contents with New and Updated specific criteria:

- The latest quick edition of the book in PDF

- The latest complete edition of the book in PDF, which criteria correspond to the criteria in...

- The Self-Assessment Excel Dashboard, and...

- Example pre-filled Self-Assessment Excel Dashboard to get familiar with results generation

- In-depth specific Checklists covering the topic

- Project management checklists and templates to assist with implementation

INCLUDES LIFETIME SELF ASSESSMENT UPDATES

Every self assessment comes with Lifetime Updates and Lifetime Free Updated Books. Lifetime Updates is an industry-first feature which allows you to receive verified self assessment updates, ensuring you always have the most accurate information at your fingertips.

Get it now- you will be glad you did - do it now, before you forget.

Send an email to **access@theartofservice.com** with this books' title in the subject to get the Request For Information Self Assessment Tool right away.

Purpose of this Self-Assessment

This Self-Assessment has been developed to improve understanding of the requirements and elements of Request For Information, based on best practices and standards in business process architecture, design and quality management.

It is designed to allow for a rapid Self-Assessment to determine how closely existing management practices and procedures correspond to the elements of the Self-Assessment.

The criteria of requirements and elements of Request For Information have been rephrased in the format of a Self-Assessment questionnaire, with a seven-criterion scoring system, as explained in this document.

In this format, even with limited background knowledge of Request For Information, a manager can quickly review existing operations to determine how they measure up to the standards. This in turn can serve as the starting point of a 'gap analysis' to identify management tools or system elements that might usefully be implemented in the organization to help improve overall performance.

How to use the Self-Assessment

On the following pages are a series of questions to identify to what extent your Request For Information initiative is complete in comparison to the requirements set in standards.

To facilitate answering the questions, there is a space in front of each question to enter a score on a scale of '1' to '5'.

1 Strongly Disagree

2 Disagree

3 Neutral

4 Agree

5 Strongly Agree

Read the question and rate it with the following in front of mind:

'In my belief, the answer to this question is clearly defined'.

There are two ways in which you can choose to interpret this statement;
1. how aware are you that the answer to the question is clearly defined
2. for more in-depth analysis you can choose to gather evidence and confirm the answer to the question. This obviously will take more time, most Self-Assessment users opt for the first way to interpret the question and dig deeper later on based on the outcome of the overall Self-Assessment.

A score of '1' would mean that the answer is not clear at all, where a '5' would mean the answer is crystal clear and defined. Leave emtpy when the question is not applicable or you don't want to answer it, you can skip it without affecting your score. Write your score in the space provided.

After you have responded to all the appropriate statements in each section, compute your average score for that section, using the formula provided, and round to the nearest tenth. Then transfer to the corresponding spoke in the Request For Information Scorecard on the second next page of the Self-Assessment.

Your completed Request For Information Scorecard will give you a clear presentation of which Request For Information areas need attention.

Request For Information
Scorecard Example

Example of how the finalized Scorecard can look like:

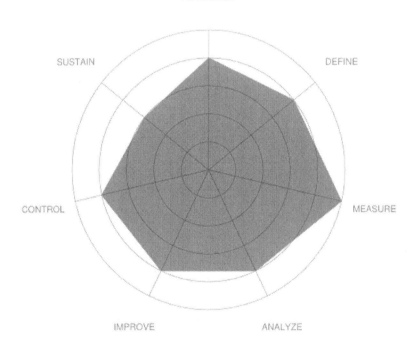

Request For Information Scorecard

Your Scores:

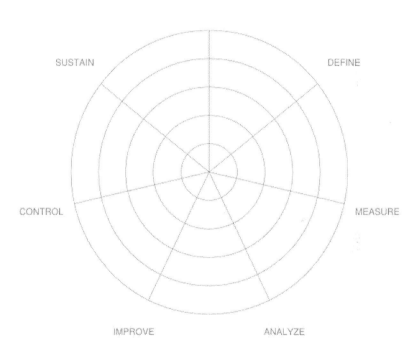

BEGINNING OF THE SELF-ASSESSMENT:

CRITERION #1: RECOGNIZE

INTENT: Be aware of the need for change. Recognize that there is an unfavorable variation, problem or symptom.

In my belief, the answer to this question is clearly defined:

5 Strongly Agree

4 Agree

3 Neutral

2 Disagree

1 Strongly Disagree

1. Will it solve real problems?
<--- Score

2. Where is training needed?
<--- Score

3. What Request for information capabilities do you need?
<--- Score

4. When a Request for information manager recognizes a problem, what options are available?
<--- Score

5. Do you have/need 24-hour access to key personnel?
<--- Score

6. Think about the people you identified for your Request for information project and the project responsibilities you would assign to them, what kind of training do you think they would need to perform these responsibilities effectively?
<--- Score

7. What is the Request for information problem definition? What do you need to resolve?
<--- Score

8. Who needs to know about Request for information?
<--- Score

9. Will new equipment/products be required to facilitate Request for information delivery, for example is new software needed?
<--- Score

10. Are there any revenue recognition issues?
<--- Score

11. What would happen if Request for information weren't done?
<--- Score

12. Does Request for information create potential

expectations in other areas that need to be recognized and considered?

<--- Score

13. Did you miss any major Request for information issues?

<--- Score

14. Who needs budgets?

<--- Score

15. What information do users need?

<--- Score

16. Why is this needed?

<--- Score

17. How do you identify the kinds of information that you will need?

<--- Score

18. Who are your key stakeholders who need to sign off?

<--- Score

19. What should be considered when identifying available resources, constraints, and deadlines?

<--- Score

20. What does Request for information success mean to the stakeholders?

<--- Score

21. What is the smallest subset of the problem you can usefully solve?

<--- Score

22. To what extent does each concerned units management team recognize Request for information as an effective investment?
<--- Score

23. Are there recognized Request for information problems?
<--- Score

24. Who needs to know?
<--- Score

25. How do you assess your Request for information workforce capability and capacity needs, including skills, competencies, and staffing levels?
<--- Score

26. What do employees need in the short term?
<--- Score

27. Will a response program recognize when a crisis occurs and provide some level of response?
<--- Score

28. What is the recognized need?
<--- Score

29. Who else hopes to benefit from it?
<--- Score

30. Are there Request for information problems defined?
<--- Score

31. What creative shifts do you need to take?

<--- Score

32. Consider your own Request for information project, what types of organizational problems do you think might be causing or affecting your problem, based on the work done so far?
<--- Score

33. What training and capacity building actions are needed to implement proposed reforms?
<--- Score

34. Are there any specific expectations or concerns about the Request for information team, Request for information itself?
<--- Score

35. What are the stakeholder objectives to be achieved with Request for information?
<--- Score

36. What are the Request for information resources needed?
<--- Score

37. How are the Request for information's objectives aligned to the group's overall stakeholder strategy?
<--- Score

38. Do you recognize Request for information achievements?
<--- Score

39. Would you recognize a threat from the inside?
<--- Score

40. Can management personnel recognize the monetary benefit of Request for information?
<--- Score

41. Have you identified your Request for information key performance indicators?
<--- Score

42. What prevents you from making the changes you know will make you a more effective Request for information leader?
<--- Score

43. Where do you need to exercise leadership?
<--- Score

44. What activities does the governance board need to consider?
<--- Score

45. For your Request for information project, identify and describe the business environment, is there more than one layer to the business environment?
<--- Score

46. Who needs what information?
<--- Score

47. How do you recognize an objection?
<--- Score

48. What is the problem or issue?
<--- Score

49. How are you going to measure success?

<--- Score

50. Who defines the rules in relation to any given issue?
<--- Score

51. Do you need different information or graphics?
<--- Score

52. How can auditing be a preventative security measure?
<--- Score

53. What tools and technologies are needed for a custom Request for information project?
<--- Score

54. What Request for information events should you attend?
<--- Score

55. Is the need for organizational change recognized?
<--- Score

56. What is the problem and/or vulnerability?
<--- Score

57. What needs to be done?
<--- Score

58. Which needs are not included or involved?
<--- Score

59. What are the timeframes required to resolve each of the issues/problems?
<--- Score

60. What Request for information coordination do you need?
<--- Score

61. Does your organization need more Request for information education?
<--- Score

62. How do you identify subcontractor relationships?
<--- Score

63. What Request for information problem should be solved?
<--- Score

64. Are there regulatory / compliance issues?
<--- Score

65. What are the clients issues and concerns?
<--- Score

66. Which information does the Request for information business case need to include?
<--- Score

67. What resources or support might you need?
<--- Score

68. How do you take a forward-looking perspective in identifying Request for information research related to market response and models?
<--- Score

69. What are the expected benefits of Request for information to the stakeholder?

<--- Score

70. What is the extent or complexity of the Request for information problem?
<--- Score

71. What needs to stay?
<--- Score

72. As a sponsor, customer or management, how important is it to meet goals, objectives?
<--- Score

73. What else needs to be measured?
<--- Score

74. How are training requirements identified?
<--- Score

75. Is the quality assurance team identified?
<--- Score

76. Do you know what you need to know about Request for information?
<--- Score

77. Are problem definition and motivation clearly presented?
<--- Score

78. Do you need to avoid or amend any Request for information activities?
<--- Score

79. How many trainings, in total, are needed?
<--- Score

80. Are losses recognized in a timely manner?
<--- Score

81. How does it fit into your organizational needs and tasks?
<--- Score

82. Whom do you really need or want to serve?
<--- Score

83. Are employees recognized or rewarded for performance that demonstrates the highest levels of integrity?
<--- Score

84. What situation(s) led to this Request for information Self Assessment?
<--- Score

85. Is it clear when you think of the day ahead of you what activities and tasks you need to complete?
<--- Score

86. Are your goals realistic? Do you need to redefine your problem? Perhaps the problem has changed or maybe you have reached your goal and need to set a new one?
<--- Score

87. Looking at each person individually – does every one have the qualities which are needed to work in this group?
<--- Score

88. Are controls defined to recognize and contain problems?
<--- Score

89. How much are sponsors, customers, partners, stakeholders involved in Request for information? In other words, what are the risks, if Request for information does not deliver successfully?
<--- Score

90. What do you need to start doing?
<--- Score

91. Who should resolve the Request for information issues?
<--- Score

92. Which issues are too important to ignore?
<--- Score

93. What problems are you facing and how do you consider Request for information will circumvent those obstacles?
<--- Score

94. How do you recognize an Request for information objection?
<--- Score

95. Why the need?
<--- Score

96. Will Request for information deliverables need to be tested and, if so, by whom?
<--- Score

Add up total points for this section:
_____ = Total points for this section

Divided by: _____ (number of
statements answered) = _____
Average score for this section

Transfer your score to the Request for
information Index at the beginning of
the Self-Assessment.

CRITERION #2: DEFINE:

INTENT: Formulate the stakeholder problem. Define the problem, needs and objectives.

In my belief, the answer to this question is clearly defined:

5 Strongly Agree

4 Agree

3 Neutral

2 Disagree

1 Strongly Disagree

1. Have specific policy objectives been defined?
<--- Score

2. Are customer(s) identified and segmented according to their different needs and requirements?
<--- Score

3. Who is gathering information?
<--- Score

4. What is the definition of Request for information excellence?
<--- Score

5. Has anyone else (internal or external to the group) attempted to solve this problem or a similar one before? If so, what knowledge can be leveraged from these previous efforts?
<--- Score

6. Has a high-level 'as is' process map been completed, verified and validated?
<--- Score

7. How do you keep key subject matter experts in the loop?
<--- Score

8. When is/was the Request for information start date?
<--- Score

9. What information should you gather?
<--- Score

10. Is scope creep really all bad news?
<--- Score

11. Are improvement team members fully trained on Request for information?
<--- Score

12. What customer feedback methods were used to solicit their input?
<--- Score

13. How and when will the baselines be defined?
<--- Score

14. What are the Roles and Responsibilities for each team member and its leadership? Where is this documented?
<--- Score

15. What baselines are required to be defined and managed?
<--- Score

16. Are customers identified and high impact areas defined?
<--- Score

17. What are the requirements for audit information?
<--- Score

18. How would you define the culture at your organization, how susceptible is it to Request for information changes?
<--- Score

19. What sort of initial information to gather?
<--- Score

20. Who are the Request for information improvement team members, including Management Leads and Coaches?
<--- Score

21. If substitutes have been appointed, have they been briefed on the Request for information goals and received regular communications as to the

progress to date?

<--- Score

22. What scope to assess?

<--- Score

23. Who is gathering Request for information information?

<--- Score

24. How does the Request for information manager ensure against scope creep?

<--- Score

25. Are there different segments of customers?

<--- Score

26. What is in scope?

<--- Score

27. Is full participation by members in regularly held team meetings guaranteed?

<--- Score

28. Are stakeholder processes mapped?

<--- Score

29. What are the rough order estimates on cost savings/opportunities that Request for information brings?

<--- Score

30. Is the Request for information scope manageable?

<--- Score

31. How do you catch Request for information

definition inconsistencies?
<--- Score

32. What is the context?
<--- Score

33. Will a Request for information production readiness review be required?
<--- Score

34. What is the scope?
<--- Score

35. In what way can you redefine the criteria of choice clients have in your category in your favor?
<--- Score

36. Has a project plan, Gantt chart, or similar been developed/completed?
<--- Score

37. How do you gather requirements?
<--- Score

38. Has the improvement team collected the 'voice of the customer' (obtained feedback – qualitative and quantitative)?
<--- Score

39. Has the Request for information work been fairly and/or equitably divided and delegated among team members who are qualified and capable to perform the work? Has everyone contributed?
<--- Score

40. Is the team formed and are team leaders (Coaches

and Management Leads) assigned?
<--- Score

41. What is in the scope and what is not in scope?
<--- Score

42. What are the dynamics of the communication plan?
<--- Score

43. Are task requirements clearly defined?
<--- Score

44. Are the Request for information requirements complete?
<--- Score

45. Has your scope been defined?
<--- Score

46. Is there regularly 100% attendance at the team meetings? If not, have appointed substitutes attended to preserve cross-functionality and full representation?
<--- Score

47. Is the current 'as is' process being followed? If not, what are the discrepancies?
<--- Score

48. What key stakeholder process output measure(s) does Request for information leverage and how?
<--- Score

49. How do you think the partners involved in Request for information would have defined success?

<--- Score

50. What are the compelling stakeholder reasons for embarking on Request for information?
<--- Score

51. Is data collected and displayed to better understand customer(s) critical needs and requirements.
<--- Score

52. How do you manage changes in Request for information requirements?
<--- Score

53. What is a worst-case scenario for losses?
<--- Score

54. What was the context?
<--- Score

55. Are roles and responsibilities formally defined?
<--- Score

56. Are team charters developed?
<--- Score

57. What happens if Request for information's scope changes?
<--- Score

58. What are the tasks and definitions?
<--- Score

59. What gets examined?
<--- Score

60. Is the team equipped with available and reliable resources?
<--- Score

61. Has the direction changed at all during the course of Request for information? If so, when did it change and why?
<--- Score

62. Is Request for information linked to key stakeholder goals and objectives?
<--- Score

63. What critical content must be communicated – who, what, when, where, and how?
<--- Score

64. Is the Request for information scope complete and appropriately sized?
<--- Score

65. Has/have the customer(s) been identified?
<--- Score

66. What defines best in class?
<--- Score

67. Who approved the Request for information scope?
<--- Score

68. How would you define Request for information leadership?
<--- Score

69. Has everyone on the team, including the team leaders, been properly trained?
<--- Score

70. Has a team charter been developed and communicated?
<--- Score

71. What is out-of-scope initially?
<--- Score

72. How did the Request for information manager receive input to the development of a Request for information improvement plan and the estimated completion dates/times of each activity?
<--- Score

73. What are the core elements of the Request for information business case?
<--- Score

74. How do you manage unclear Request for information requirements?
<--- Score

75. How do you gather the stories?
<--- Score

76. What sources do you use to gather information for a Request for information study?
<--- Score

77. How will the Request for information team and the group measure complete success of Request for information?
<--- Score

78. Are resources adequate for the scope?
<--- Score

79. What intelligence can you gather?
<--- Score

80. How can the value of Request for information be defined?
<--- Score

81. When is the estimated completion date?
<--- Score

82. Have the customer needs been translated into specific, measurable requirements? How?
<--- Score

83. How do you hand over Request for information context?
<--- Score

84. What is the definition of success?
<--- Score

85. Are different versions of process maps needed to account for the different types of inputs?
<--- Score

86. What is the scope of the Request for information work?
<--- Score

87. Do you have a Request for information success story or case study ready to tell and share?
<--- Score

88. Are there any constraints known that bear on the ability to perform Request for information work? How is the team addressing them?

<--- Score

89. What are the Request for information tasks and definitions?

<--- Score

90. Are approval levels defined for contracts and supplements to contracts?

<--- Score

91. Is special Request for information user knowledge required?

<--- Score

92. Why are you doing Request for information and what is the scope?

<--- Score

93. Are all requirements met?

<--- Score

94. Is there a completed SIPOC representation, describing the Suppliers, Inputs, Process, Outputs, and Customers?

<--- Score

95. Are required metrics defined, what are they?

<--- Score

96. What system do you use for gathering Request for information information?

<--- Score

97. Is there a Request for information management charter, including stakeholder case, problem and goal statements, scope, milestones, roles and responsibilities, communication plan?
<--- Score

98. What knowledge or experience is required?
<--- Score

99. The political context: who holds power?
<--- Score

100. Does the team have regular meetings?
<--- Score

101. Will team members perform Request for information work when assigned and in a timely fashion?
<--- Score

102. Is it clearly defined in and to your organization what you do?
<--- Score

103. How will variation in the actual durations of each activity be dealt with to ensure that the expected Request for information results are met?
<--- Score

104. What would be the goal or target for a Request for information's improvement team?
<--- Score

105. What constraints exist that might impact the team?

<--- Score

106. What is the scope of Request for information?
<--- Score

107. Who defines (or who defined) the rules and roles?
<--- Score

108. What is the worst case scenario?
<--- Score

109. Is the team sponsored by a champion or stakeholder leader?
<--- Score

110. How do you gather Request for information requirements?
<--- Score

111. Where can you gather more information?
<--- Score

112. Is Request for information currently on schedule according to the plan?
<--- Score

113. Is there a critical path to deliver Request for information results?
<--- Score

114. Have all of the relationships been defined properly?
<--- Score

115. What are (control) requirements for Request for information Information?

<--- Score

116. How often are the team meetings?
<--- Score

117. Are audit criteria, scope, frequency and methods defined?
<--- Score

118. Are accountability and ownership for Request for information clearly defined?
<--- Score

119. How was the 'as is' process map developed, reviewed, verified and validated?
<--- Score

120. Is the improvement team aware of the different versions of a process: what they think it is vs. what it actually is vs. what it should be vs. what it could be?
<--- Score

121. Do the problem and goal statements meet the SMART criteria (specific, measurable, attainable, relevant, and time-bound)?
<--- Score

122. When are meeting minutes sent out? Who is on the distribution list?
<--- Score

123. Are the Request for information requirements testable?
<--- Score

124. How have you defined all Request for

information requirements first?

<--- Score

125. Do you all define Request for information in the same way?

<--- Score

126. How do you manage scope?

<--- Score

127. Is there a completed, verified, and validated high-level 'as is' (not 'should be' or 'could be') stakeholder process map?

<--- Score

128. Do you have organizational privacy requirements?

<--- Score

129. What is the scope of the Request for information effort?

<--- Score

130. What scope do you want your strategy to cover?

<--- Score

131. What is out of scope?

<--- Score

132. What Request for information requirements should be gathered?

<--- Score

133. Scope of sensitive information?

<--- Score

134. Is the team adequately staffed with the desired cross-functionality? If not, what additional resources are available to the team?
<--- Score

135. Will team members regularly document their Request for information work?
<--- Score

136. Has a Request for information requirement not been met?
<--- Score

137. How do you build the right business case?
<--- Score

138. Is the scope of Request for information defined?
<--- Score

139. What specifically is the problem? Where does it occur? When does it occur? What is its extent?
<--- Score

140. What are the boundaries of the scope? What is in bounds and what is not? What is the start point? What is the stop point?
<--- Score

141. How is the team tracking and documenting its work?
<--- Score

142. Does the scope remain the same?
<--- Score

Add up total points for this section:
_____ = Total points for this section

Divided by: _____ (number of
statements answered) = _____
Average score for this section

Transfer your score to the Request for
information Index at the beginning of
the Self-Assessment.

CRITERION #3: MEASURE:

INTENT: Gather the correct data.
Measure the current performance and
evolution of the situation.

In my belief, the answer to this
question is clearly defined:

5 Strongly Agree

4 Agree

3 Neutral

2 Disagree

1 Strongly Disagree

1. Is there an opportunity to verify requirements?
<--- Score

2. What is your decision requirements diagram?
<--- Score

3. What are the costs?
<--- Score

4. What are the Request for information key cost drivers?

<--- Score

5. What tests verify requirements?

<--- Score

6. What is your Request for information quality cost segregation study?

<--- Score

7. Does the Request for information task fit the client's priorities?

<--- Score

8. How much does it cost?

<--- Score

9. How sensitive must the Request for information strategy be to cost?

<--- Score

10. Where can you go to verify the info?

<--- Score

11. What evidence is there and what is measured?

<--- Score

12. What are allowable costs?

<--- Score

13. Where is it measured?

<--- Score

14. Are you able to realize any cost savings?

<--- Score

15. What is the cost of rework?
<--- Score

16. What measurements are being captured?
<--- Score

17. Who should receive measurement reports?
<--- Score

18. What does verifying compliance entail?
<--- Score

19. How to cause the change?
<--- Score

20. How is the value delivered by Request for information being measured?
<--- Score

21. What happens if cost savings do not materialize?
<--- Score

22. Why a Request for information focus?
<--- Score

23. What is the total cost related to deploying Request for information, including any consulting or professional services?
<--- Score

24. What are hidden Request for information quality costs?
<--- Score

25. What relevant entities could be measured?
<--- Score

26. How can you manage cost down?
<--- Score

27. Are supply costs steady or fluctuating?
<--- Score

28. What are the costs of reform?
<--- Score

29. Was a business case (cost/benefit) developed?
<--- Score

30. Did you tackle the cause or the symptom?
<--- Score

31. When a disaster occurs, who gets priority?
<--- Score

32. How do you verify if Request for information is built right?
<--- Score

33. How are measurements made?
<--- Score

34. How do you measure lifecycle phases?
<--- Score

35. When are costs are incurred?
<--- Score

36. What does your operating model cost?
<--- Score

37. Are missed Request for information opportunities costing your organization money?
<--- Score

38. How do you focus on what is right -not who is right?
<--- Score

39. How do you measure efficient delivery of Request for information services?
<--- Score

40. Do you verify that corrective actions were taken?
<--- Score

41. What does losing customers cost your organization?
<--- Score

42. What are your primary costs, revenues, assets?
<--- Score

43. Are there measurements based on task performance?
<--- Score

44. Will Request for information have an impact on current business continuity, disaster recovery processes and/or infrastructure?
<--- Score

45. Does management have the right priorities among projects?
<--- Score

46. Are indirect costs charged to the Request for information program?

<--- Score

47. How is progress measured?

<--- Score

48. How will effects be measured?

<--- Score

49. Have you made assumptions about the shape of the future, particularly its impact on your customers and competitors?

<--- Score

50. How do you verify performance?

<--- Score

51. What are the Request for information investment costs?

<--- Score

52. Is the solution cost-effective?

<--- Score

53. Have design-to-cost goals been established?

<--- Score

54. How can a Request for information test verify your ideas or assumptions?

<--- Score

55. Do you effectively measure and reward individual and team performance?

<--- Score

56. Why do you expend time and effort to implement measurement, for whom?
<--- Score

57. Are the units of measure consistent?
<--- Score

58. What harm might be caused?
<--- Score

59. What are the current costs of the Request for information process?
<--- Score

60. What is an unallowable cost?
<--- Score

61. What potential environmental factors impact the Request for information effort?
<--- Score

62. What can be used to verify compliance?
<--- Score

63. How will success or failure be measured?
<--- Score

64. How do you control the overall costs of your work processes?
<--- Score

65. What could cause you to change course?
<--- Score

66. How do you measure variability?
<--- Score

67. Who is involved in verifying compliance?
<--- Score

68. How do you verify and develop ideas and innovations?
<--- Score

69. What is the Request for information business impact?
<--- Score

70. How can you reduce costs?
<--- Score

71. How will measures be used to manage and adapt?
<--- Score

72. What does a Test Case verify?
<--- Score

73. Does a Request for information quantification method exist?
<--- Score

74. Who pays the cost?
<--- Score

75. What would it cost to replace your technology?
<--- Score

76. How frequently do you verify your Request for information strategy?
<--- Score

77. Are you aware of what could cause a problem?

<--- Score

78. Do the benefits outweigh the costs?
<--- Score

79. Are Request for information vulnerabilities categorized and prioritized?
<--- Score

80. How will your organization measure success?
<--- Score

81. Have you included everything in your Request for information cost models?
<--- Score

82. Is it possible to estimate the impact of unanticipated complexity such as wrong or failed assumptions, feedback, etcetera on proposed reforms?
<--- Score

83. What causes mismanagement?
<--- Score

84. What causes innovation to fail or succeed in your organization?
<--- Score

85. What do people want to verify?
<--- Score

86. What drives O&M cost?
<--- Score

87. What are your customers expectations and

measures?
<--- Score

88. How do you verify Request for information completeness and accuracy?
<--- Score

89. How do you aggregate measures across priorities?
<--- Score

90. What is the cause of any Request for information gaps?
<--- Score

91. At what cost?
<--- Score

92. Which Request for information impacts are significant?
<--- Score

93. Which costs should be taken into account?
<--- Score

94. What are the estimated costs of proposed changes?
<--- Score

95. Do you aggressively reward and promote the people who have the biggest impact on creating excellent Request for information services/products?
<--- Score

96. What are your operating costs?
<--- Score

97. How frequently do you track Request for information measures?
<--- Score

98. What could cause delays in the schedule?
<--- Score

99. Do you have any cost Request for information limitation requirements?
<--- Score

100. How do you verify your resources?
<--- Score

101. What causes investor action?
<--- Score

102. Among the Request for information product and service cost to be estimated, which is considered hardest to estimate?
<--- Score

103. How can you measure the performance?
<--- Score

104. How do you prevent mis-estimating cost?
<--- Score

105. Do you have an issue in getting priority?
<--- Score

106. Do you have a flow diagram of what happens?
<--- Score

107. Are there any easy-to-implement alternatives to Request for information? Sometimes other solutions

are available that do not require the cost implications of a full-blown project?

<--- Score

108. How can you measure Request for information in a systematic way?

<--- Score

109. Are there competing Request for information priorities?

<--- Score

110. What disadvantage does this cause for the user?

<--- Score

111. What users will be impacted?

<--- Score

112. How do you measure success?

<--- Score

113. Are the measurements objective?

<--- Score

114. Are actual costs in line with budgeted costs?

<--- Score

115. What are the operational costs after Request for information deployment?

<--- Score

116. When should you bother with diagrams?

<--- Score

117. How are you verifying it?

<--- Score

118. What are the strategic priorities for this year?
<--- Score

119. Is the cost worth the Request for information effort ?
<--- Score

120. Which measures and indicators matter?
<--- Score

121. What are the uncertainties surrounding estimates of impact?
<--- Score

122. What are the types and number of measures to use?
<--- Score

123. How is performance measured?
<--- Score

124. How do you quantify and qualify impacts?
<--- Score

125. Are the Request for information benefits worth its costs?
<--- Score

126. How do you verify and validate the Request for information data?
<--- Score

127. How do you verify the authenticity of the data and information used?
<--- Score

128. What measurements are possible, practicable and meaningful?
<--- Score

129. Are you taking your company in the direction of better and revenue or cheaper and cost?
<--- Score

130. What do you measure and why?
<--- Score

131. How will costs be allocated?
<--- Score

132. What are the costs and benefits?
<--- Score

133. How do you verify the Request for information requirements quality?
<--- Score

134. What methods are feasible and acceptable to estimate the impact of reforms?
<--- Score

135. What is measured? Why?
<--- Score

136. What details are required of the Request for information cost structure?
<--- Score

137. The approach of traditional Request for information works for detail complexity but is focused on a systematic approach rather than an

understanding of the nature of systems themselves, what approach will permit your organization to deal with the kind of unpredictable emergent behaviors that dynamic complexity can introduce?
<--- Score

138. How do your measurements capture actionable Request for information information for use in exceeding your customers expectations and securing your customers engagement?
<--- Score

139. What are your key Request for information organizational performance measures, including key short and longer-term financial measures?
<--- Score

140. What are the costs of delaying Request for information action?
<--- Score

141. Has a cost center been established?
<--- Score

Add up total points for this section:
_ _ _ _ _ = Total points for this section

Divided by: _ _ _ _ _ _ (number of statements answered) = _ _ _ _ _ _
Average score for this section

Transfer your score to the Request for information Index at the beginning of the Self-Assessment.

CRITERION #4: ANALYZE:

INTENT: Analyze causes, assumptions
and hypotheses.

In my belief, the answer to this
question is clearly defined:

5 Strongly Agree

4 Agree

3 Neutral

2 Disagree

1 Strongly Disagree

1. What is the Request for information Driver?
<--- Score

2. What is the cost of poor quality as supported by the team's analysis?
<--- Score

3. How are outputs preserved and protected?
<--- Score

4. What qualifications are necessary?

<--- Score

5. What is your organizations system for selecting qualified vendors?

<--- Score

6. Do your employees have the opportunity to do what they do best everyday?

<--- Score

7. What Request for information data will be collected?

<--- Score

8. Do you, as a leader, bounce back quickly from setbacks?

<--- Score

9. What does the data say about the performance of the stakeholder process?

<--- Score

10. What are your outputs?

<--- Score

11. What are your key performance measures or indicators and in-process measures for the control and improvement of your Request for information processes?

<--- Score

12. What data do you need to collect?

<--- Score

13. Is data and process analysis, root cause analysis

and quantifying the gap/opportunity in place?
<--- Score

14. Is the final output clearly identified?
<--- Score

15. Are you missing Request for information opportunities?
<--- Score

16. How was the detailed process map generated, verified, and validated?
<--- Score

17. How many input/output points does it require?
<--- Score

18. How difficult is it to qualify what Request for information ROI is?
<--- Score

19. Is the required Request for information data gathered?
<--- Score

20. What qualifications and skills do you need?
<--- Score

21. What data is gathered?
<--- Score

22. Did any value-added analysis or 'lean thinking' take place to identify some of the gaps shown on the 'as is' process map?
<--- Score

23. How is the Request for information Value Stream Mapping managed?
<--- Score

24. Where can you get qualified talent today?
<--- Score

25. What types of data do your Request for information indicators require?
<--- Score

26. Is the suppliers process defined and controlled?
<--- Score

27. Who will gather what data?
<--- Score

28. What resources go in to get the desired output?
<--- Score

29. Were any designed experiments used to generate additional insight into the data analysis?
<--- Score

30. Have the problem and goal statements been updated to reflect the additional knowledge gained from the analyze phase?
<--- Score

31. What is the complexity of the output produced?
<--- Score

32. What will drive Request for information change?
<--- Score

33. Think about some of the processes you undertake within your organization, which do you own?
<--- Score

34. What other organizational variables, such as reward systems or communication systems, affect the performance of this Request for information process?
<--- Score

35. What qualifies as competition?
<--- Score

36. What did the team gain from developing a sub-process map?
<--- Score

37. How will the Request for information data be captured?
<--- Score

38. How does the organization define, manage, and improve its Request for information processes?
<--- Score

39. How do you promote understanding that opportunity for improvement is not criticism of the status quo, or the people who created the status quo?
<--- Score

40. What kind of crime could a potential new hire have committed that would not only not disqualify him/her from being hired by your organization,

but would actually indicate that he/she might be a particularly good fit?
<--- Score

41. What are the necessary qualifications?
<--- Score

42. What is the Value Stream Mapping?
<--- Score

43. Have any additional benefits been identified that will result from closing all or most of the gaps?
<--- Score

44. What process improvements will be needed?
<--- Score

45. What are the processes for audit reporting and management?
<--- Score

46. Did any additional data need to be collected?
<--- Score

47. How do you ensure that the Request for information opportunity is realistic?
<--- Score

48. What is the output?
<--- Score

49. Who gets your output?
<--- Score

50. What qualifications are needed?
<--- Score

51. What are evaluation criteria for the output?
<--- Score

52. What successful thing are you doing today that may be blinding you to new growth opportunities?
<--- Score

53. An organizationally feasible system request is one that considers the mission, goals and objectives of the organization, key questions are: is the Request for information solution request practical and will it solve a problem or take advantage of an opportunity to achieve company goals?
<--- Score

54. How has the Request for information data been gathered?
<--- Score

55. Are your outputs consistent?
<--- Score

56. Is pre-qualification of suppliers carried out?
<--- Score

57. Who is involved with workflow mapping?
<--- Score

58. What methods do you use to gather Request for information data?
<--- Score

59. Should you invest in industry-recognized qualifications?
<--- Score

60. What quality tools were used to get through the analyze phase?
<--- Score

61. Is the gap/opportunity displayed and communicated in financial terms?
<--- Score

62. What are the revised rough estimates of the financial savings/opportunity for Request for information improvements?
<--- Score

63. Were Pareto charts (or similar) used to portray the 'heavy hitters' (or key sources of variation)?
<--- Score

64. What output to create?
<--- Score

65. Identify an operational issue in your organization, for example, could a particular task be done more quickly or more efficiently by Request for information?
<--- Score

66. How do you identify specific Request for information investment opportunities and emerging trends?
<--- Score

67. Have you defined which data is gathered how?
<--- Score

68. How often will data be collected for measures?
<--- Score

69. What are your current levels and trends in key measures or indicators of Request for information product and process performance that are important to and directly serve your customers? How do these results compare with the performance of your competitors and other organizations with similar offerings?
<--- Score

70. What are the Request for information business drivers?
<--- Score

71. How do you define collaboration and team output?
<--- Score

72. What internal processes need improvement?
<--- Score

73. How do you measure the operational performance of your key work systems and processes, including productivity, cycle time, and other appropriate measures of process effectiveness, efficiency, and innovation?
<--- Score

74. Are all team members qualified for all tasks?
<--- Score

75. Were there any improvement opportunities identified from the process analysis?
<--- Score

76. Is the Request for information process severely

broken such that a re-design is necessary?
<--- Score

77. Has data output been validated?
<--- Score

78. What Request for information metrics are outputs of the process?
<--- Score

79. Do staff qualifications match your project?
<--- Score

80. How do mission and objectives affect the Request for information processes of your organization?
<--- Score

81. Which Request for information data should be retained?
<--- Score

82. What training and qualifications will you need?
<--- Score

83. What are the personnel training and qualifications required?
<--- Score

84. What are your best practices for minimizing Request for information project risk, while demonstrating incremental value and quick wins throughout the Request for information project lifecycle?
<--- Score

85. What were the crucial 'moments of truth' on the

process map?

<--- Score

86. What conclusions were drawn from the team's data collection and analysis? How did the team reach these conclusions?

<--- Score

87. How do you use Request for information data and information to support organizational decision making and innovation?

<--- Score

88. What tools were used to generate the list of possible causes?

<--- Score

89. Do quality systems drive continuous improvement?

<--- Score

90. What were the financial benefits resulting from any 'ground fruit or low-hanging fruit' (quick fixes)?

<--- Score

91. Are all staff in core Request for information subjects Highly Qualified?

<--- Score

92. Who owns what data?

<--- Score

93. Do several people in different organizational units assist with the Request for information process?

<--- Score

94. How can risk management be tied procedurally to process elements?
<--- Score

95. How is the way you as the leader think and process information affecting your organizational culture?
<--- Score

96. How will the change process be managed?
<--- Score

97. What, related to, Request for information processes does your organization outsource?
<--- Score

98. Do your contracts/agreements contain data security obligations?
<--- Score

99. What are the best opportunities for value improvement?
<--- Score

100. How do your work systems and key work processes relate to and capitalize on your core competencies?
<--- Score

101. Who is involved in the management review process?
<--- Score

102. Do you have the authority to produce the output?
<--- Score

103. How will the data be checked for quality?
<--- Score

104. What is your organizations process which leads to recognition of value generation?
<--- Score

105. What information qualified as important?
<--- Score

106. What are your current levels and trends in key Request for information measures or indicators of product and process performance that are important to and directly serve your customers?
<--- Score

107. Is there a strict change management process?
<--- Score

108. What other jobs or tasks affect the performance of the steps in the Request for information process?
<--- Score

109. What qualifications do Request for information leaders need?
<--- Score

110. What tools were used to narrow the list of possible causes?
<--- Score

111. How will corresponding data be collected?
<--- Score

112. Are Request for information changes recognized

early enough to be approved through the regular process?

<--- Score

113. Has an output goal been set?

<--- Score

114. What Request for information data should be collected?

<--- Score

115. Is the performance gap determined?

<--- Score

116. What Request for information data should be managed?

<--- Score

117. What process should you select for improvement?

<--- Score

118. How much data can be collected in the given timeframe?

<--- Score

119. Is there any way to speed up the process?

<--- Score

120. Record-keeping requirements flow from the records needed as inputs, outputs, controls and for transformation of a Request for information process, are the records needed as inputs to the Request for information process available?

<--- Score

121. Was a detailed process map created to amplify critical steps of the 'as is' stakeholder process?
<--- Score

122. Do you understand your management processes today?
<--- Score

123. Can you add value to the current Request for information decision-making process (largely qualitative) by incorporating uncertainty modeling (more quantitative)?
<--- Score

124. Are gaps between current performance and the goal performance identified?
<--- Score

125. How do you implement and manage your work processes to ensure that they meet design requirements?
<--- Score

126. What are your Request for information processes?
<--- Score

127. How is Request for information data gathered?
<--- Score

128. Do your leaders quickly bounce back from setbacks?
<--- Score

129. Was a cause-and-effect diagram used to explore the different types of causes (or sources of variation)?
<--- Score

130. What are the disruptive Request for information technologies that enable your organization to radically change your business processes?
<--- Score

131. A compounding model resolution with available relevant data can often provide insight towards a solution methodology; which Request for information models, tools and techniques are necessary?
<--- Score

132. Where is Request for information data gathered?
<--- Score

Add up total points for this section:
_ _ _ _ _ = Total points for this section

Divided by: _ _ _ _ _ _ (number of statements answered) = _ _ _ _ _ _
Average score for this section

Transfer your score to the Request for information Index at the beginning of the Self-Assessment.

CRITERION #5: IMPROVE:

INTENT: Develop a practical solution. Innovate, establish and test the solution and to measure the results.

In my belief, the answer to this question is clearly defined:

5 Strongly Agree

4 Agree

3 Neutral

2 Disagree

1 Strongly Disagree

1. What were the underlying assumptions on the cost-benefit analysis?
<--- Score

2. Do you combine technical expertise with business knowledge and Request for information Key topics include lifecycles, development approaches, requirements and how to make a business case?
<--- Score

3. Do vendor agreements bring new compliance risk ?
<--- Score

4. What tools were used to evaluate the potential solutions?
<--- Score

5. How do you measure improved Request for information service perception, and satisfaction?
<--- Score

6. What strategies for Request for information improvement are successful?
<--- Score

7. How does your organization evaluate strategic Request for information success?
<--- Score

8. What are your current levels and trends in key measures or indicators of workforce and leader development?
<--- Score

9. What criteria will you use to assess your Request for information risks?
<--- Score

10. How can you better manage risk?
<--- Score

11. How will you measure the results?
<--- Score

12. What should a proof of concept or pilot

accomplish?
<--- Score

13. Who makes the Request for information decisions in your organization?
<--- Score

14. Is the optimal solution selected based on testing and analysis?
<--- Score

15. What risks do you need to manage?
<--- Score

16. What can you do to improve?
<--- Score

17. What attendant changes will need to be made to ensure that the solution is successful?
<--- Score

18. What to do with the results or outcomes of measurements?
<--- Score

19. Who do you report Request for information results to?
<--- Score

20. Do those selected for the Request for information team have a good general understanding of what Request for information is all about?
<--- Score

21. What resources are required for the improvement efforts?

<--- Score

22. What is the Request for information's sustainability risk?
<--- Score

23. How will you recognize and celebrate results?
<--- Score

24. What communications are necessary to support the implementation of the solution?
<--- Score

25. How do you deal with Request for information risk?
<--- Score

26. How will you know when its improved?
<--- Score

27. What tools were used to tap into the creativity and encourage 'outside the box' thinking?
<--- Score

28. What current systems have to be understood and/or changed?
<--- Score

29. What is the implementation plan?
<--- Score

30. Is the implementation plan designed?
<--- Score

31. Are risk management tasks balanced centrally and locally?

<--- Score

32. How are Request for information risks managed?
<--- Score

33. What are the affordable Request for information risks?
<--- Score

34. What practices helps your organization to develop its capacity to recognize patterns?
<--- Score

35. Is there a high likelihood that any recommendations will achieve their intended results?
<--- Score

36. How do you define the solutions' scope?
<--- Score

37. How do you improve your likelihood of success ?
<--- Score

38. Are decisions made in a timely manner?
<--- Score

39. How risky is your organization?
<--- Score

40. Risk events: what are the things that could go wrong?
<--- Score

41. What needs improvement? Why?
<--- Score

42. How is knowledge sharing about risk management improved?

<--- Score

43. Is the measure of success for Request for information understandable to a variety of people?

<--- Score

44. What lessons, if any, from a pilot were incorporated into the design of the full-scale solution?

<--- Score

45. Is there a cost/benefit analysis of optimal solution(s)?

<--- Score

46. How do you mitigate Request for information risk?

<--- Score

47. Who do you report Request for information results to?

<--- Score

48. What tools do you use once you have decided on a Request for information strategy and more importantly how do you choose?

<--- Score

49. Is the solution technically practical?

<--- Score

50. How is continuous improvement applied to risk management?

<--- Score

51. Is risk periodically assessed?

<--- Score

52. What is Request for information's impact on utilizing the best solution(s)?
<--- Score

53. How will you know that a change is an improvement?
<--- Score

54. Do you have the optimal project management team structure?
<--- Score

55. Where do the Request for information decisions reside?
<--- Score

56. What do you want to improve?
<--- Score

57. Was a pilot designed for the proposed solution(s)?
<--- Score

58. To what extent does management recognize Request for information as a tool to increase the results?
<--- Score

59. What improvements have been achieved?
<--- Score

60. Which Request for information solution is appropriate?
<--- Score

61. Was a Request for information charter developed?
<--- Score

62. Does the goal represent a desired result that can be measured?
<--- Score

63. Is the Request for information solution sustainable?
<--- Score

64. Who will be responsible for documenting the Request for information requirements in detail?
<--- Score

65. What Request for information improvements can be made?
<--- Score

66. Have you identified breakpoints and/or risk tolerances that will trigger broad consideration of a potential need for intervention or modification of strategy?
<--- Score

67. What are the Request for information security risks?
<--- Score

68. What does the 'should be' process map/design look like?
<--- Score

69. Risk Identification: What are the possible risk events your organization faces in relation to Request for information?

<--- Score

70. How do you improve Request for information service perception, and satisfaction?
<--- Score

71. Can the solution be designed and implemented within an acceptable time period?
<--- Score

72. How do you decide how much to remunerate an employee?
<--- Score

73. What are the implications of the one critical Request for information decision 10 minutes, 10 months, and 10 years from now?
<--- Score

74. How do you keep improving Request for information?
<--- Score

75. Who manages supplier risk management in your organization?
<--- Score

76. How do you measure risk?
<--- Score

77. Who controls the risk?
<--- Score

78. What is the team's contingency plan for potential problems occurring in implementation?
<--- Score

79. Why improve in the first place?
<--- Score

80. Are the risks fully understood, reasonable and manageable?
<--- Score

81. At what point will vulnerability assessments be performed once Request for information is put into production (e.g., ongoing Risk Management after implementation)?
<--- Score

82. What error proofing will be done to address some of the discrepancies observed in the 'as is' process?
<--- Score

83. In the past few months, what is the smallest change you have made that has had the biggest positive result? What was it about that small change that produced the large return?
<--- Score

84. What is the risk?
<--- Score

85. How can you improve performance?
<--- Score

86. Who manages Request for information risk?
<--- Score

87. What are the concrete Request for information results?
<--- Score

88. What actually has to improve and by how much?
<--- Score

89. Is any Request for information documentation required?
<--- Score

90. Is there any other Request for information solution?
<--- Score

91. Which of the recognised risks out of all risks can be most likely transferred?
<--- Score

92. Can you integrate quality management and risk management?
<--- Score

93. How do you go about comparing Request for information approaches/solutions?
<--- Score

94. Who should make the Request for information decisions?
<--- Score

95. Who will be responsible for making the decisions to include or exclude requested changes once Request for information is underway?
<--- Score

96. Is the scope clearly documented?
<--- Score

97. Is the Request for information risk managed?

<--- Score

98. Request for information risk decisions: whose call
Is It?

<--- Score

99. Are procedures documented for managing
Request for information risks?

<--- Score

**100. Risk factors: what are the characteristics of
Request for information that make it risky?**

<--- Score

101. Does a good decision guarantee a good
outcome?

<--- Score

102. How scalable is your Request for information
solution?

<--- Score

**103. How do you manage and improve your
Request for information work systems to deliver
customer value and achieve organizational
success and sustainability?**

<--- Score

104. If you could go back in time five years, what
decision would you make differently? What is your
best guess as to what decision you're making today
you might regret five years from now?

<--- Score

105. How significant is the improvement in the eyes of the end user?
<--- Score

106. Is pilot data collected and analyzed?
<--- Score

107. What are the expected Request for information results?
<--- Score

108. Are risk triggers captured?
<--- Score

109. How do you manage Request for information risk?
<--- Score

110. Can you identify any significant risks or exposures to Request for information third-parties (vendors, service providers, alliance partners etc) that concern you?
<--- Score

111. For decision problems, how do you develop a decision statement?
<--- Score

112. What were the criteria for evaluating a Request for information pilot?
<--- Score

113. How will you know that you have improved?
<--- Score

114. Is supporting Request for information

documentation required?

<--- Score

115. How do the Request for information results compare with the performance of your competitors and other organizations with similar offerings?

<--- Score

116. Who are the Request for information decision makers?

<--- Score

117. Is there a small-scale pilot for proposed improvement(s)? What conclusions were drawn from the outcomes of a pilot?

<--- Score

118. Who controls key decisions that will be made?

<--- Score

119. How can the phases of Request for information development be identified?

<--- Score

120. How do you measure progress and evaluate training effectiveness?

<--- Score

121. Is the Request for information documentation thorough?

<--- Score

122. For estimation problems, how do you develop an estimation statement?

<--- Score

123. What went well, what should change, what can improve?
<--- Score

124. How does the team improve its work?
<--- Score

125. How can you improve Request for information?
<--- Score

126. Where do you need Request for information improvement?
<--- Score

127. Who are the key stakeholders for the Request for information evaluation?
<--- Score

128. What is the magnitude of the improvements?
<--- Score

129. Were any criteria developed to assist the team in testing and evaluating potential solutions?
<--- Score

130. Are the most efficient solutions problem-specific?
<--- Score

131. What tools were most useful during the improve phase?
<--- Score

132. Are events managed to resolution?
<--- Score

133. Who will be using the results of the measurement

activities?
<--- Score

134. Explorations of the frontiers of Request for information will help you build influence, improve Request for information, optimize decision making, and sustain change, what is your approach?
<--- Score

135. Do you cover the five essential competencies: Communication, Collaboration,Innovation, Adaptability, and Leadership that improve an organizations ability to leverage the new Request for information in a volatile global economy?
<--- Score

136. When you map the key players in your own work and the types/domains of relationships with them, which relationships do you find easy and which challenging, and why?
<--- Score

137. Who are the Request for information decision-makers?
<--- Score

Add up total points for this section:
_____ = Total points for this section

Divided by: _____ (number of statements answered) = _____
Average score for this section

Transfer your score to the Request for information Index at the beginning of the Self-Assessment.

CRITERION #6: CONTROL:

INTENT: Implement the practical solution. Maintain the performance and correct possible complications.

In my belief, the answer to this question is clearly defined:

5 Strongly Agree

4 Agree

3 Neutral

2 Disagree

1 Strongly Disagree

1. Can you adapt and adjust to changing Request for information situations?
<--- Score

2. How will the process owner verify improvement in present and future sigma levels, process capabilities?
<--- Score

3. What are your results for key measures or

indicators of the accomplishment of your Request for information strategy and action plans, including building and strengthening core competencies?
<--- Score

4. Will your goals reflect your program budget?
<--- Score

5. What do you measure to verify effectiveness gains?
<--- Score

6. Who controls critical resources?
<--- Score

7. How do controls support value?
<--- Score

8. What quality tools were useful in the control phase?
<--- Score

9. Is there a recommended audit plan for routine surveillance inspections of Request for information's gains?
<--- Score

10. How will you measure your QA plan's effectiveness?
<--- Score

11. Who sets the Request for information standards?
<--- Score

12. How do you establish and deploy modified action plans if circumstances require a shift in plans and rapid execution of new plans?

<--- Score

13. How do you plan on providing proper recognition and disclosure of supporting companies?
<--- Score

14. Does the Request for information performance meet the customer's requirements?
<--- Score

15. What are the known security controls?
<--- Score

16. Does a troubleshooting guide exist or is it needed?
<--- Score

17. How might the group capture best practices and lessons learned so as to leverage improvements?
<--- Score

18. What other areas of the group might benefit from the Request for information team's improvements, knowledge, and learning?
<--- Score

19. What should the next improvement project be that is related to Request for information?
<--- Score

20. Has the Request for information value of standards been quantified?
<--- Score

21. What is the recommended frequency of auditing?
<--- Score

22. Is the Request for information test/monitoring cost justified?

<--- Score

23. Do the Request for information decisions you make today help people and the planet tomorrow?

<--- Score

24. You may have created your quality measures at a time when you lacked resources, technology wasn't up to the required standard, or low service levels were the industry norm. Have those circumstances changed?

<--- Score

25. What do you stand for--and what are you against?

<--- Score

26. Implementation Planning: is a pilot needed to test the changes before a full roll out occurs?

<--- Score

27. How will input, process, and output variables be checked to detect for sub-optimal conditions?

<--- Score

28. How will the day-to-day responsibilities for monitoring and continual improvement be transferred from the improvement team to the process owner?

<--- Score

29. How do you plan for the cost of succession?

<--- Score

30. How can you best use all of your knowledge repositories to enhance learning and sharing?
<--- Score

31. What are you attempting to measure/monitor?
<--- Score

32. How do you monitor usage and cost?
<--- Score

33. What is the control/monitoring plan?
<--- Score

34. How will Request for information decisions be made and monitored?
<--- Score

35. Are pertinent alerts monitored, analyzed and distributed to appropriate personnel?
<--- Score

36. Is there a transfer of ownership and knowledge to process owner and process team tasked with the responsibilities.
<--- Score

37. What adjustments to the strategies are needed?
<--- Score

38. Is there documentation that will support the successful operation of the improvement?
<--- Score

39. Does the response plan contain a definite closed loop continual improvement scheme (e.g., plan-do-check-act)?

<--- Score

40. Does job training on the documented procedures need to be part of the process team's education and training?
<--- Score

41. Are the planned controls in place?
<--- Score

42. How is Request for information project cost planned, managed, monitored?
<--- Score

43. Have new or revised work instructions resulted?
<--- Score

44. What are the performance and scale of the Request for information tools?
<--- Score

45. Do the viable solutions scale to future needs?
<--- Score

46. What key inputs and outputs are being measured on an ongoing basis?
<--- Score

47. Is new knowledge gained imbedded in the response plan?
<--- Score

48. Act/Adjust: What Do you Need to Do Differently?
<--- Score

49. What do your reports reflect?

<--- Score

50. How widespread is its use?
<--- Score

51. Is reporting being used or needed?
<--- Score

52. Does Request for information appropriately measure and monitor risk?
<--- Score

53. Are you measuring, monitoring and predicting Request for information activities to optimize operations and profitability, and enhancing outcomes?
<--- Score

54. What other systems, operations, processes, and infrastructures (hiring practices, staffing, training, incentives/rewards, metrics/dashboards/scorecards, etc.) need updates, additions, changes, or deletions in order to facilitate knowledge transfer and improvements?
<--- Score

55. Is a response plan established and deployed?
<--- Score

56. Has the improved process and its steps been standardized?
<--- Score

57. Are the Request for information standards challenging?
<--- Score

58. How do your controls stack up?
<--- Score

59. How will the process owner and team be able to hold the gains?
<--- Score

60. What can you control?
<--- Score

61. Is there an action plan in case of emergencies?
<--- Score

62. How will report readings be checked to effectively monitor performance?
<--- Score

63. Is there a standardized process?
<--- Score

64. How do senior leaders actions reflect a commitment to the organizations Request for information values?
<--- Score

65. What is your plan to assess your security risks?
<--- Score

66. Is a response plan in place for when the input, process, or output measures indicate an 'out-of-control' condition?
<--- Score

67. Will existing staff require re-training, for example, to learn new business processes?

<--- Score

68. Are suggested corrective/restorative actions indicated on the response plan for known causes to problems that might surface?
<--- Score

69. What Request for information standards are applicable?
<--- Score

70. Is there a documented and implemented monitoring plan?
<--- Score

71. How will new or emerging customer needs/requirements be checked/communicated to orient the process toward meeting the new specifications and continually reducing variation?
<--- Score

72. How do you encourage people to take control and responsibility?
<--- Score

73. Will any special training be provided for results interpretation?
<--- Score

74. Is there a control plan in place for sustaining improvements (short and long-term)?
<--- Score

75. Where do ideas that reach policy makers and planners as proposals for Request for information strengthening and reform actually originate?

<--- Score

76. Who will be in control?
<--- Score

77. Who is going to spread your message?
<--- Score

78. What should you measure to verify efficiency gains?
<--- Score

79. Is knowledge gained on process shared and institutionalized?
<--- Score

80. In the case of a Request for information project, the criteria for the audit derive from implementation objectives, an audit of a Request for information project involves assessing whether the recommendations outlined for implementation have been met, can you track that any Request for information project is implemented as planned, and is it working?
<--- Score

81. What is the standard for acceptable Request for information performance?
<--- Score

82. What is your theory of human motivation, and how does your compensation plan fit with that view?
<--- Score

83. How likely is the current Request for information plan to come in on schedule or on

budget?
<--- Score

84. What are the critical parameters to watch?
<--- Score

85. Who is the Request for information process owner?
<--- Score

86. Are documented procedures clear and easy to follow for the operators?
<--- Score

87. Can support from partners be adjusted?
<--- Score

88. Is there a Request for information Communication plan covering who needs to get what information when?
<--- Score

89. Against what alternative is success being measured?
<--- Score

90. Do you monitor the Request for information decisions made and fine tune them as they evolve?
<--- Score

91. Are new process steps, standards, and documentation ingrained into normal operations?
<--- Score

92. Are operating procedures consistent?
<--- Score

93. Who has control over resources?
<--- Score

94. How do you select, collect, align, and integrate Request for information data and information for tracking daily operations and overall organizational performance, including progress relative to strategic objectives and action plans?
<--- Score

95. Are there documented procedures?
<--- Score

96. How do you spread information?
<--- Score

97. How is change control managed?
<--- Score

98. Do you monitor the effectiveness of your Request for information activities?
<--- Score

99. Are controls in place and consistently applied?
<--- Score

Add up total points for this section:
_ _ _ _ _ = Total points for this section

Divided by: _ _ _ _ _ _ (number of statements answered) = _ _ _ _ _ _
Average score for this section

Transfer your score to the Request for information Index at the beginning of

the Self-Assessment.

CRITERION #7: SUSTAIN:

INTENT: Retain the benefits.

In my belief, the answer to this
question is clearly defined:

5 Strongly Agree

4 Agree

3 Neutral

2 Disagree

1 Strongly Disagree

1. Who do we want your customers to become?
<--- Score

2. What could happen if you do not do it?
<--- Score

3. Do you say no to customers for no reason?
<--- Score

4. What do we do when new problems arise?
<--- Score

5. To whom do you add value?
<--- Score

6. What are the long-term Request for information goals?
<--- Score

7. How do you stay inspired?
<--- Score

8. What is the source of the strategies for Request for information strengthening and reform?
<--- Score

9. How much contingency will be available in the budget?
<--- Score

10. Is your basic point _____ or _____?
<--- Score

11. What is the kind of project structure that would be appropriate for your Request for information project, should it be formal and complex, or can it be less formal and relatively simple?
<--- Score

12. Why should people listen to you?
<--- Score

13. Were lessons learned captured and communicated?
<--- Score

14. If there were zero limitations, what would you do

differently?
<--- Score

15. Who will determine interim and final deadlines?
<--- Score

16. Who is responsible for Request for information?
<--- Score

17. Can you do all this work?
<--- Score

18. Who else should you help?
<--- Score

19. How do you foster innovation?
<--- Score

20. How do you listen to customers to obtain
actionable information?
<--- Score

21. Have new benefits been realized?
<--- Score

22. What trophy do you want on your mantle?
<--- Score

**23. What potential megatrends could make your
business model obsolete?**
<--- Score

24. What is the recommended frequency of auditing?
<--- Score

25. How much does Request for information help?

<--- Score

26. How do you maintain Request for information's Integrity?
<--- Score

27. Who have you, as a company, historically been when you've been at your best?
<--- Score

28. Who is responsible for ensuring appropriate resources (time, people and money) are allocated to Request for information?
<--- Score

29. What are the rules and assumptions your industry operates under? What if the opposite were true?
<--- Score

30. If your customer were your grandmother, would you tell her to buy what you're selling?
<--- Score

31. What is your competitive advantage?
<--- Score

32. What are current Request for information paradigms?
<--- Score

33. Ask yourself: how would you do this work if you only had one staff member to do it?
<--- Score

34. Is a Request for information team work effort in place?

<--- Score

35. At what moment would you think; Will I get fired?
<--- Score

36. Who is the main stakeholder, with ultimate responsibility for driving Request for information forward?
<--- Score

37. Political -is anyone trying to undermine this project?
<--- Score

38. Which Request for information goals are the most important?
<--- Score

39. Are you / should you be revolutionary or evolutionary?
<--- Score

40. Which models, tools and techniques are necessary?
<--- Score

41. In retrospect, of the projects that you pulled the plug on, what percent do you wish had been allowed to keep going, and what percent do you wish had ended earlier?
<--- Score

42. Who do you think the world wants your organization to be?
<--- Score

43. What one word do you want to own in the minds of your customers, employees, and partners?

<--- Score

44. What is the big Request for information idea?

<--- Score

45. Do you think Request for information accomplishes the goals you expect it to accomplish?

<--- Score

46. Who will provide the final approval of Request for information deliverables?

<--- Score

47. What is an unauthorized commitment?

<--- Score

48. What is your question? Why?

<--- Score

49. What is the overall business strategy?

<--- Score

50. How do you make it meaningful in connecting Request for information with what users do day-to-day?

<--- Score

51. Is a Request for information breakthrough on the horizon?

<--- Score

52. How do you lead with Request for information in mind?

<--- Score

53. How do you provide a safe environment -physically and emotionally?
<--- Score

54. What unique value proposition (UVP) do you offer?
<--- Score

55. Will there be any necessary staff changes (redundancies or new hires)?
<--- Score

56. How important is Request for information to the user organizations mission?
<--- Score

57. What is your BATNA (best alternative to a negotiated agreement)?
<--- Score

58. What is the overall talent health of your organization as a whole at senior levels, and for each organization reporting to a member of the Senior Leadership Team?
<--- Score

59. How will you ensure you get what you expected?
<--- Score

60. If you had to rebuild your organization without any traditional competitive advantages (i.e., no killer technology, promising research, innovative product/service delivery model, etcetera), how would your people have to approach their work

and collaborate together in order to create the necessary conditions for success?

<--- Score

61. What have been your experiences in defining long range Request for information goals?

<--- Score

62. Which individuals, teams or departments will be involved in Request for information?

<--- Score

63. How is implementation research currently incorporated into each of your goals?

<--- Score

64. Are your responses positive or negative?

<--- Score

65. How can you become more high-tech but still be high touch?

<--- Score

66. How do you accomplish your long range Request for information goals?

<--- Score

67. Are you relevant? Will you be relevant five years from now? Ten?

<--- Score

68. Do you have past Request for information successes?

<--- Score

69. What information is critical to your organization

that your executives are ignoring?
<--- Score

70. Is Request for information dependent on the successful delivery of a current project?
<--- Score

71. Are there any activities that you can take off your to do list?
<--- Score

72. Why will customers want to buy your organizations products/services?
<--- Score

73. What are your most important goals for the strategic Request for information objectives?
<--- Score

74. What happens at your organization when people fail?
<--- Score

75. Can the schedule be done in the given time?
<--- Score

76. What is something you believe that nearly no one agrees with you on?
<--- Score

77. What would have to be true for the option on the table to be the best possible choice?
<--- Score

78. What goals did you miss?
<--- Score

79. How are you doing compared to your industry?
<--- Score

80. If no one would ever find out about your accomplishments, how would you lead differently?
<--- Score

81. What should you stop doing?
<--- Score

82. Is Request for information realistic, or are you setting yourself up for failure?
<--- Score

83. What are the usability implications of Request for information actions?
<--- Score

84. What will be the consequences to the stakeholder (financial, reputation etc) if Request for information does not go ahead or fails to deliver the objectives?
<--- Score

85. How do you know if you are successful?
<--- Score

86. Are the assumptions believable and achievable?
<--- Score

87. What are the essentials of internal Request for information management?
<--- Score

88. What you are going to do to affect the numbers?
<--- Score

89. How do customers see your organization?
<--- Score

90. Is there a work around that you can use?
<--- Score

91. What Request for information modifications can you make work for you?
<--- Score

92. How can you negotiate Request for information successfully with a stubborn boss, an irate client, or a deceitful coworker?
<--- Score

93. If you find that you havent accomplished one of the goals for one of the steps of the Request for information strategy, what will you do to fix it?
<--- Score

94. What are your personal philosophies regarding Request for information and how do they influence your work?
<--- Score

95. What stupid rule would you most like to kill?
<--- Score

96. What Request for information skills are most important?
<--- Score

97. What are strategies for increasing support and reducing opposition?
<--- Score

98. What are the potential basics of Request for information fraud?

<--- Score

99. How will you know that the Request for information project has been successful?

<--- Score

100. What are the challenges?

<--- Score

101. How does Request for information integrate with other stakeholder initiatives?

<--- Score

102. What knowledge, skills and characteristics mark a good Request for information project manager?

<--- Score

103. What was the last experiment you ran?

<--- Score

104. What did you miss in the interview for the worst hire you ever made?

<--- Score

105. Are new benefits received and understood?

<--- Score

106. Do you know who is a friend or a foe?

<--- Score

107. Who will manage the integration of tools?

<--- Score

108. What are internal and external Request for information relations?

<--- Score

109. How do you go about securing Request for information?

<--- Score

110. How do you govern and fulfill your societal responsibilities?

<--- Score

111. Do you think you know, or do you know you know ?

<--- Score

112. How do you set Request for information stretch targets and how do you get people to not only participate in setting these stretch targets but also that they strive to achieve these?

<--- Score

113. Think of your Request for information project, what are the main functions?

<--- Score

114. What new services of functionality will be implemented next with Request for information ?

<--- Score

115. What is effective Request for information?

<--- Score

116. Will it be accepted by users?

<--- Score

117. How do you cross-sell and up-sell your Request for information success?

<--- Score

118. What are the gaps in your knowledge and experience?

<--- Score

119. How do you determine the key elements that affect Request for information workforce satisfaction, how are these elements determined for different workforce groups and segments?

<--- Score

120. Is the impact that Request for information has shown?

<--- Score

121. How do you track customer value, profitability or financial return, organizational success, and sustainability?

<--- Score

122. What are the business goals Request for information is aiming to achieve?

<--- Score

123. Are all key stakeholders present at all Structured Walkthroughs?

<--- Score

124. Instead of going to current contacts for new ideas, what if you reconnected with dormant contacts--the people you used to know? If you were going reactivate a dormant tie, who would it be?

<--- Score

125. What counts that you are not counting?
<--- Score

126. Who are four people whose careers you have enhanced?
<--- Score

127. Marketing budgets are tighter, consumers are more skeptical, and social media has changed forever the way we talk about Request for information, how do you gain traction?
<--- Score

128. Do you have the right people on the bus?
<--- Score

129. Operational - will it work?
<--- Score

130. Are the criteria for selecting recommendations stated?
<--- Score

131. What threat is Request for information addressing?
<--- Score

132. Who is responsible for errors?
<--- Score

133. Whom among your colleagues do you trust, and for what?
<--- Score

134. Is there any reason to believe the opposite of my current belief?

<--- Score

135. Are you making progress, and are you making progress as Request for information leaders?

<--- Score

136. What happens when a new employee joins the organization?

<--- Score

137. Can you break it down?

<--- Score

138. Whose voice (department, ethnic group, women, older workers, etc) might you have missed hearing from in your company, and how might you amplify this voice to create positive momentum for your business?

<--- Score

139. What is the range of capabilities?

<--- Score

140. How will you insure seamless interoperability of Request for information moving forward?

<--- Score

141. What is the funding source for this project?

<--- Score

142. Who uses your product in ways you never expected?

<--- Score

143. What management system can you use to leverage the Request for information experience, ideas, and concerns of the people closest to the work to be done?
<--- Score

144. What is the purpose of Request for information in relation to the mission?
<--- Score

145. Who is on the team?
<--- Score

146. Who, on the executive team or the board, has spoken to a customer recently?
<--- Score

147. How likely is it that a customer would recommend your company to a friend or colleague?
<--- Score

148. Are assumptions made in Request for information stated explicitly?
<--- Score

149. How do you ensure that implementations of Request for information products are done in a way that ensures safety?
<--- Score

150. What relationships among Request for information trends do you perceive?
<--- Score

151. Can you maintain your growth without detracting from the factors that have contributed

to your success?
<--- Score

152. Do you know what you are doing? And who do you call if you don't?
<--- Score

153. What are the top 3 things at the forefront of your Request for information agendas for the next 3 years?
<--- Score

154. Do you feel that more should be done in the Request for information area?
<--- Score

155. Why not do Request for information?
<--- Score

156. How can you incorporate support to ensure safe and effective use of Request for information into the services that you provide?
<--- Score

157. What may be the consequences for the performance of an organization if all stakeholders are not consulted regarding Request for information?
<--- Score

158. Is there any existing Request for information governance structure?
<--- Score

159. In a project to restructure Request for information outcomes, which stakeholders would you involve?

<--- Score

160. Are you maintaining a past–present–future perspective throughout the Request for information discussion?
<--- Score

161. Who do you want your customers to become?
<--- Score

162. What projects are going on in the organization today, and what resources are those projects using from the resource pools?
<--- Score

163. What are specific Request for information rules to follow?
<--- Score

164. What have you done to protect your business from competitive encroachment?
<--- Score

165. How do you keep records, of what?
<--- Score

166. What would you recommend your friend do if he/she were facing this dilemma?
<--- Score

167. Who will be responsible for deciding whether Request for information goes ahead or not after the initial investigations?
<--- Score

168. Are you satisfied with your current role? If

not, what is missing from it?

<--- Score

169. Is your strategy driving your strategy? Or is the way in which you allocate resources driving your strategy?

<--- Score

170. Which functions and people interact with the supplier and or customer?

<--- Score

171. How will you motivate the stakeholders with the least vested interest?

<--- Score

172. How do you deal with Request for information changes?

<--- Score

173. How can you become the company that would put you out of business?

<--- Score

174. What trouble can you get into?

<--- Score

175. Do you see more potential in people than they do in themselves?

<--- Score

176. Where can you break convention?

<--- Score

177. If you were responsible for initiating and implementing major changes in your organization,

what steps might you take to ensure acceptance of those changes?

<--- Score

178. Who are the key stakeholders?

<--- Score

179. Do Request for information rules make a reasonable demand on a users capabilities?

<--- Score

180. Are you using a design thinking approach and integrating Innovation, Request for information Experience, and Brand Value?

<--- Score

181. How do you manage Request for information Knowledge Management (KM)?

<--- Score

182. If you do not follow, then how to lead?

<--- Score

183. What business benefits will Request for information goals deliver if achieved?

<--- Score

184. Do you have an implicit bias for capital investments over people investments?

<--- Score

185. What is your formula for success in Request for information ?

<--- Score

186. What is a feasible sequencing of reform initiatives

over time?

<--- Score

187. Do you have enough freaky customers in your portfolio pushing you to the limit day in and day out?

<--- Score

188. Is it economical; do you have the time and money?

<--- Score

189. Why should you adopt a Request for information framework?

<--- Score

190. What is it like to work for you?

<--- Score

191. What are the key enablers to make this Request for information move?

<--- Score

192. Would you rather sell to knowledgeable and informed customers or to uninformed customers?

<--- Score

193. How do you transition from the baseline to the target?

<--- Score

194. How do you proactively clarify deliverables and Request for information quality expectations?

<--- Score

195. What is the estimated value of the project?

<--- Score

196. Why is it important to have senior management support for a Request for information project?
<--- Score

197. Why do and why don't your customers like your organization?
<--- Score

198. If you had to leave your organization for a year and the only communication you could have with employees/colleagues was a single paragraph, what would you write?
<--- Score

199. Are you paying enough attention to the partners your company depends on to succeed?
<--- Score

200. When information truly is ubiquitous, when reach and connectivity are completely global, when computing resources are infinite, and when a whole new set of impossibilities are not only possible, but happening, what will that do to your business?
<--- Score

201. Who are your customers?
<--- Score

202. Have benefits been optimized with all key stakeholders?
<--- Score

203. How do you engage the workforce, in addition to satisfying them?
<--- Score

204. Do you have the right capabilities and capacities?
<--- Score

205. If you got fired and a new hire took your place, what would she do different?
<--- Score

206. What must you excel at?
<--- Score

207. If your company went out of business tomorrow, would anyone who doesn't get a paycheck here care?
<--- Score

208. How do senior leaders deploy your organizations vision and values through your leadership system, to the workforce, to key suppliers and partners, and to customers and other stakeholders, as appropriate?
<--- Score

209. How do you assess the Request for information pitfalls that are inherent in implementing it?
<--- Score

210. What role does communication play in the success or failure of a Request for information project?
<--- Score

211. Has implementation been effective in reaching specified objectives so far?
<--- Score

212. How do you keep the momentum going?
<--- Score

213. What are the short and long-term Request for information goals?
<--- Score

214. In the past year, what have you done (or could you have done) to increase the accurate perception of your company/brand as ethical and honest?
<--- Score

215. What does your signature ensure?
<--- Score

216. What is your Request for information strategy?
<--- Score

217. What are you trying to prove to yourself, and how might it be hijacking your life and business success?
<--- Score

Add up total points for this section:
_ _ _ _ _ = Total points for this section

Divided by: _ _ _ _ _ _ (number of statements answered) = _ _ _ _ _ _
Average score for this section

Transfer your score to the Request for information Index at the beginning of the Self-Assessment.

Request For Information and Managing Projects, Criteria for Project Managers:

1.0 Initiating Process Group: Request For Information

1. In which Request For Information project management process group is the detailed Request For Information project budget created?

2. What will you do to minimize the impact should a risk event occur?

3. What is the NEXT thing to do?

4. Who is performing the work of the Request For Information project?

5. During which stage of Risk planning are modeling techniques used to determine overall effects of risks on Request For Information project objectives for high probability, high impact risks?

6. What must be done?

7. Do you know if the Request For Information project requires outside equipment or vendor resources?

8. What input will you be required to provide the Request For Information project team?

9. Do you understand the quality and control criteria that must be achieved for successful Request For Information project completion?

10. The process to Manage Stakeholders is part of which process group?

11. Establishment of pm office?

12. Although the Request For Information project manager does not directly manage procurement and contracting activities, who does manage procurement and contracting activities in your organization then if not the PM?

13. The Request For Information project you are managing has nine stakeholders. How many channel of communications are there between corresponding stakeholders?

14. What technical work to do in each phase?

15. At which stage, in a typical Request For Information project do stake holders have maximum influence?

16. Are you certain deliverables are properly completed and meet quality standards?

17. Were decisions made in a timely manner?

18. Which six sigma dmaic phase focuses on why and how defects and errors occur?

19. What will you do?

20. Are identified risks being monitored properly, are new risks arising during the Request For Information project or are foreseen risks occurring?

1.1 Project Charter: Request For Information

21. Why have you chosen the aim you have set forth?

22. What are the deliverables?

23. What barriers do you predict to your success?

24. Fit with other Products Compliments – Cannibalizes?

25. Are you building in-house ?

26. How high should you set your goals?

27. What metrics could you look at?

28. Dependent Request For Information projects: what Request For Information projects must be underway or completed before this Request For Information project can be successful?

29. For whom?

30. Why do you need to manage scope?

31. Pop quiz – which are the same inputs as in the Request For Information project charter?

32. How will you learn more about the process or system you are trying to improve?

33. Customer: who are you doing the Request For Information project for?

34. What ideas do you have for initial tests of change (PDSA cycles)?

35. If finished, on what date did it finish?

36. Who is the sponsor?

37. Name and describe the elements that deal with providing the detail?

38. How will you know a change is an improvement?

39. Is time of the essence?

40. When will this occur?

1.2 Stakeholder Register: Request For Information

41. Is your organization ready for change?

42. How big is the gap?

43. Who are the stakeholders?

44. What is the power of the stakeholder?

45. Who is managing stakeholder engagement?

46. How much influence do they have on the Request For Information project?

47. What & Why?

48. How should employers make voices heard?

49. What opportunities exist to provide communications?

50. What are the major Request For Information project milestones requiring communications or providing communications opportunities?

51. How will reports be created?

52. Who wants to talk about Security?

1.3 Stakeholder Analysis Matrix: Request For Information

53. Partnerships, agencies, distribution?

54. What is in it for you?

55. Political effects?

56. Continuity, supply chain robustness?

57. Partnership opportunities/synergies?

58. Technology development and innovation?

59. Accreditations, etc?

60. What should thwe organizations stakeholders avoid?

61. Insurmountable weaknesses?

62. How are you predicting what future (work)loads will be?

63. Who has not been involved up to now and should have been?

64. Sustainable financial backing?

65. What are the opportunities for communication?

66. How to measure the achievement of the

Immediate Objective?

67. Tactics: eg, surprise, major contracts?

68. What can the stakeholder prevent from happening?

69. What unique or lowest-cost resources does the Request For Information project have access to?

70. Industry or lifestyle trends?

71. Cultural, attitudinal, behavioural?

72. What is the stakeholders name, what is function?

2.0 Planning Process Group: Request For Information

73. Contingency planning. if a risk event occurs, what will you do?

74. What good practices or successful experiences or transferable examples have been identified?

75. What are the different approaches to building the WBS?

76. What do you need to do?

77. How should needs be met?

78. What factors are contributing to progress or delay in the achievement of products and results?

79. Is the pace of implementing the products of the program ensuring the completeness of the results of the Request For Information project?

80. You are creating your WBS and find that you keep decomposing tasks into smaller and smaller units. How can you tell when you are done?

81. If a task is partitionable, is this a sufficient condition to reduce the Request For Information project duration?

82. To what extent are the visions and actions of the partners consistent or divergent with regard to the

program?

83. In which Request For Information project management process group is the detailed Request For Information project budget created?

84. Professionals want to know what is expected from them; what are the deliverables?

85. To what extent are the participating departments coordinating with each other?

86. Explanation: is what the Request For Information project intents to solve a hard question?

87. How are the principles of aid effectiveness (ownership, alignment, management for development results and mutual responsibility) being applied in the Request For Information project?

88. Who are the Request For Information project stakeholders?

89. To what extent has a PMO contributed to raising the quality of the design of the Request For Information project?

90. Is the Request For Information project supported by national and/or local organizations?

91. What types of differentiated effects are resulting from the Request For Information project and to what extent?

92. What business situation is being addressed?

2.1 Project Management Plan: Request For Information

93. What would you do differently?

94. When is the Request For Information project management plan created?

95. Why do you manage integration?

96. What is Request For Information project scope management?

97. Are comparable cost estimates used for comparing, screening and selecting alternative plans, and has a reasonable cost estimate been developed for the recommended plan?

98. Is there an incremental analysis/cost effectiveness analysis of proposed mitigation features based on an approved method and using an accepted model?

99. Will you add a schedule and diagram?

100. Where does all this information come from?

101. Is mitigation authorized or recommended?

102. What if, for example, the positive direction and vision of your organization causes expected trends to change resulting in greater need than expected?

103. What did not work so well?

104. Has the selected plan been formulated using cost effectiveness and incremental analysis techniques?

105. What is the business need?

106. What worked well?

107. What are the constraints?

108. Is the budget realistic?

109. Are the existing and future without-plan conditions reasonable and appropriate?

110. Are there any windfall benefits that would accrue to the Request For Information project sponsor or other parties?

111. Did the planning effort collaborate to develop solutions that integrate expertise, policies, programs, and Request For Information projects across entities?

2.2 Scope Management Plan: Request For Information

112. Has adequate time for orientation & training of Request For Information project staff been provided for in relation to technical nature of the application and the experience levels of Request For Information project personnel?

113. Are mitigation strategies identified?

114. Have all unresolved risks been documented?

115. What went wrong?

116. Are Request For Information project team members involved in detailed estimating and scheduling?

117. Is there a formal set of procedures supporting Issues Management?

118. Are funding resource estimates sufficiently detailed and documented for use in planning and tracking the Request For Information project?

119. Time estimation – how much time will be needed?

120. What do you need to do to accomplish the goal or goals?

121. Are there checklists created to demine if all

quality processes are followed?

122. Is there any form of automated support for Issues Management?

123. Is there a Request For Information project organization chart showing the reporting relationships and responsibilities for each position?

124. What are the risks that could significantly affect the communication on the Request For Information project?

125. Assess the expected stability of the scope of this Request For Information project how likely is it to change, how frequently, and by how much?

126. Do you secure formal approval of changes and requirements from stakeholders?

127. Does the Request For Information project team have the skills necessary to successfully complete current Request For Information project(s) and support the application?

128. Are actuals compared against estimates to analyze and correct variances?

129. Was the scope definition used in task sequencing?

130. Are procurement deliverables arriving on time and to specification?

131. Can the Request For Information project team do several activities in parallel?

2.3 Requirements Management Plan: Request For Information

132. Is there formal agreement on who has authority to approve a change in requirements?

133. Subject to change control?

134. Did you avoid subjective, flowery or non-specific statements?

135. Do you expect stakeholders to be cooperative?

136. Do you have price sheets and a methodology for determining the total proposal cost?

137. Do you have an agreed upon process for alerting the Request For Information project Manager if a request for change in requirements leads to a product scope change?

138. Is stakeholder risk tolerance an important factor for the requirements process in this Request For Information project?

139. Are actual resources expenditures versus planned expenditures acceptable?

140. How will the requirements become prioritized?

141. Who is responsible for quantifying the Request For Information project requirements?

142. Is any organizational data being used or stored?

143. After the requirements are gathered and set forth on the requirements register, theyre little more than a laundry list of items. Some may be duplicates, some might conflict with others and some will be too broad or too vague to understand. Describe how the requirements will be analyzed. Who will perform the analysis?

144. Is it new or replacing an existing business system or process?

145. How will the information be distributed?

146. Who will do the reporting and to whom will reports be delivered?

147. What cost metrics will be used?

148. What is a problem?

149. Which hardware or software, related to, or as outcome of the Request For Information project is new to your organization?

150. How will unresolved questions be handled once approval has been obtained?

151. Will you document changes to requirements?

2.4 Requirements Documentation: Request For Information

152. Completeness. are all functions required by the customer included?

153. How will requirements be documented and who signs off on them?

154. How will they be documented / shared?

155. Who provides requirements?

156. Where do you define what is a customer, what are the attributes of customer?

157. What if the system wasn t implemented?

158. Are there legal issues?

159. Basic work/business process; high-level, what is being touched?

160. If applicable; are there issues linked with the fact that this is an offshore Request For Information project?

161. How does the proposed Request For Information project contribute to the overall objectives of your organization?

162. What is the risk associated with the technology?

163. Is your business case still valid?

164. What are the potential disadvantages/ advantages?

165. What marketing channels do you want to use: e-mail, letter or sms?

166. What kind of entity is a problem ?

167. How will the proposed Request For Information project help?

168. Does your organization restrict technical alternatives?

169. How to document system requirements?

170. What will be the integration problems?

171. Verifiability. can the requirements be checked?

2.5 Requirements Traceability Matrix: Request For Information

172. Is there a requirements traceability process in place?

173. Why use a WBS?

174. What is the WBS?

175. How small is small enough?

176. What percentage of Request For Information projects are producing traceability matrices between requirements and other work products?

177. How do you manage scope?

178. Will you use a Requirements Traceability Matrix?

179. How will it affect the stakeholders personally in career?

180. Describe the process for approving requirements so they can be added to the traceability matrix and Request For Information project work can be performed. Will the Request For Information project requirements become approved in writing?

181. Why do you manage scope?

182. Do you have a clear understanding of all subcontracts in place?

183. What are the chronologies, contingencies, consequences, criteria?

2.6 Project Scope Statement: Request For Information

184. Will tasks be marked complete only after QA has been successfully completed?

185. Have you been able to easily identify success criteria and create objective measurements for each of the Request For Information project scopes goal statements?

186. Will this process be communicated to the customer and Request For Information project team?

187. Are there backup strategies for key members of the Request For Information project?

188. Is the Request For Information project manager qualified and experienced in Request For Information project management?

189. If you were to write a list of what should not be included in the scope statement, what are the things that you would recommend be described as out-of-scope?

190. Is your organization structure appropriate for the Request For Information projects size and complexity?

191. Will the risk plan be updated on a regular and frequent basis?

192. Elements of scope management that deal with

concept development ?

193. Will the risk status be reported to management on a regular and frequent basis?

194. Were key Request For Information project stakeholders brought into the Request For Information project Plan?

195. What went right?

196. Have the configuration management functions been assigned?

197. Is the quality function identified and assigned?

198. Will statistics related to QA be collected, trends analyzed, and problems raised as issues?

199. Was planning completed before the Request For Information project was initiated?

200. Are there specific processes you will use to evaluate and approve/reject changes?

201. Request For Information project lead, team lead, solution architect?

202. Has the format for tracking and monitoring schedules and costs been defined?

203. Are there completion/verification criteria defined for each task producing an output?

2.7 Assumption and Constraint Log: Request For Information

204. Does the traceability documentation describe the tool and/or mechanism to be used to capture traceability throughout the life cycle?

205. Do documented requirements exist for all critical components and areas, including technical, business, interfaces, performance, security and conversion requirements?

206. Are requirements management tracking tools and procedures in place?

207. Are there nonconformance issues?

208. What do you log?

209. Have all necessary approvals been obtained?

210. Violation trace: why ?

211. What is positive about the current process?

212. Does the system design reflect the requirements?

213. Does a specific action and/or state that is known to violate security policy occur?

214. Are there standards for code development?

215. How many Request For Information project staff

does this specific process affect?

216. What does an audit system look like?

217. Are there unnecessary steps that are creating bottlenecks and/or causing people to wait?

218. What weaknesses do you have?

219. What strengths do you have?

220. What do you audit?

221. Model-building: what data-analytic strategies are useful when building proportional-hazards models?

222. How relevant is this attribute to this Request For Information project or audit?

223. Are there ways to reduce the time it takes to get something approved?

2.8 Work Breakdown Structure: Request For Information

224. How big is a work-package?

225. Where does it take place?

226. What has to be done?

227. When do you stop?

228. When would you develop a Work Breakdown Structure?

229. How far down?

230. How much detail?

231. Do you need another level?

232. Can you make it?

233. Is the work breakdown structure (wbs) defined and is the scope of the Request For Information project clear with assigned deliverable owners?

234. How many levels?

235. Why is it useful?

236. Who has to do it?

237. Why would you develop a Work Breakdown

Structure?

238. What is the probability that the Request For Information project duration will exceed xx weeks?

239. How will you and your Request For Information project team define the Request For Information projects scope and work breakdown structure?

240. When does it have to be done?

241. Is it still viable?

2.9 WBS Dictionary: Request For Information

242. Are data elements summarized through the functional organizational structure for progressively higher levels of management?

243. Are overhead budgets and costs being handled according to the disclosure statement when applicable, or otherwise properly classified (for example, engineering overhead, IR&D)?

244. Is the anticipated (firm and potential) business base Request For Information projected in a rational, consistent manner?

245. Are indirect costs charged to the appropriate indirect pools and incurring organization?

246. Software specification, development, integration, and testing, licenses ?

247. Are records maintained to show how management reserves are used?

248. Budgets assigned to control accounts?

249. Are meaningful indicators identified for use in measuring the status of cost and schedule performance?

250. Are overhead costs budgets established on a basis consistent with anticipated direct business

base?

251. Identify and isolate causes of favorable and unfavorable cost and schedule variances?

252. Does the cost accumulation system provide for summarization of indirect costs from the point of allocation to the contract total?

253. Identify potential or actual overruns and underruns?

254. Contractor financial periods; for example, annual?

255. Does the contractors system provide for the determination of cost variances attributable to the excess usage of material?

256. Is authorization of budgets in excess of the contract budget base controlled formally and done with the full knowledge and recognition of the procuring activity?

257. Does the contractors system include procedures for measuring the performance of critical subcontractors?

258. Actual cost of work performed?

2.10 Schedule Management Plan: Request For Information

259. Is the critical path valid?

260. Does the schedule have reasonable float?

261. Are Request For Information project team members involved in detailed estimating and scheduling?

262. Timeline and milestones?

263. Are vendor invoices audited for accuracy before payment?

264. Define units of measurement for each resource. For example, are you referencing gallons or liters?

265. Were the budget estimates reasonable?

266. Personnel with expertise?

267. Is quality monitored from the perspective of the customers needs and expectations?

268. Does the business case include how the Request For Information project aligns with your organizations strategic goals & objectives?

269. Does the time Request For Information projection include an amount for contingencies (time reserves)?

270. Were Request For Information project team members involved in the development of activity & task decomposition?

271. Will the Request For Information project sponsor be involved in preliminary schedule reviews?

272. How relevant is this attribute to this Request For Information project or audit?

273. Is there an on-going process in place to monitor Request For Information project risks?

274. Has process improvement efforts been completed before requirements efforts begin?

275. Has your organization readiness assessment been conducted?

276. Is a process defined to measure the performance of the schedule management process itself?

2.11 Activity List: Request For Information

277. How difficult will it be to do specific activities on this Request For Information project?

278. What is the probability the Request For Information project can be completed in xx weeks?

279. What are the critical bottleneck activities?

280. Is infrastructure setup part of your Request For Information project?

281. The wbs is developed as part of a joint planning session. and how do you know that youhave done this right?

282. What are you counting on?

283. Where will it be performed?

284. Can you determine the activity that must finish, before this activity can start?

285. How should ongoing costs be monitored to try to keep the Request For Information project within budget?

286. When will the work be performed?

287. What did not go as well?

288. What is the total time required to complete the Request For Information project if no delays occur?

289. Are the required resources available or need to be acquired?

290. In what sequence?

291. How can the Request For Information project be displayed graphically to better visualize the activities?

292. How detailed should a Request For Information project get?

293. What will be performed?

294. What is the LF and LS for each activity?

2.12 Activity Attributes: Request For Information

295. What is missing?

296. Have you identified the Activity Leveling Priority code value on each activity?

297. How else could the items be grouped?

298. Have constraints been applied to the start and finish milestones for the phases?

299. Are the required resources available?

300. Activity: fair or not fair?

301. Resource is assigned to?

302. Does your organization of the data change its meaning?

303. How do you manage time?

304. Is there anything planned that does not need to be here?

305. Why?

306. How difficult will it be to complete specific activities on this Request For Information project?

307. Do you feel very comfortable with your

prediction?

308. Can more resources be added?

309. Activity: what is Missing?

310. Were there other ways you could have organized the data to achieve similar results?

311. How many days do you need to complete the work scope with a limit of X number of resources?

312. What activity do you think you should spend the most time on?

2.13 Milestone List: Request For Information

313. What is your organizations history in doing similar activities?

314. What date will the task finish?

315. How will the milestone be verified?

316. Describe the concept of the technology, product or service that will be or has been developed. How will it be used?

317. Reliability of data, plan predictability?

318. Who will manage the Request For Information project on a day-to-day basis?

319. Timescales, deadlines and pressures?

320. How late can the activity start?

321. What has been done so far?

322. Sustaining internal capabilities?

323. How difficult will it be to do specific activities on this Request For Information project?

324. What is the market for your technology, product or service?

325. Global influences?

326. Legislative effects?

327. What background experience, skills, and strengths does the team bring to your organization?

328. What would happen if a delivery of material was one week late?

329. Identify critical paths (one or more) and which activities are on the critical path?

2.14 Network Diagram: Request For Information

330. Can you calculate the confidence level?

331. What are the Key Success Factors?

332. How confident can you be in your milestone dates and the delivery date?

333. Where do schedules come from?

334. Planning: who, how long, what to do?

335. Where do you schedule uncertainty time?

336. If the Request For Information project network diagram cannot change and you have extra personnel resources, what is the BEST thing to do?

337. What is the probability of completing the Request For Information project in less that xx days?

338. What is the completion time?

339. Exercise: what is the probability that the Request For Information project duration will exceed xx weeks?

340. What activities must occur simultaneously with this activity?

341. What controls the start and finish of a job?

342. Why must you schedule milestones, such as reviews, throughout the Request For Information project?

343. Are you on time?

344. Review the logical flow of the network diagram. Take a look at which activities you have first and then sequence the activities. Do they make sense?

345. What can be done concurrently?

346. What job or jobs could run concurrently?

2.15 Activity Resource Requirements: Request For Information

347. Do you use tools like decomposition and rolling-wave planning to produce the activity list and other outputs?

348. How many signatures do you require on a check and does this match what is in your policy and procedures?

349. Other support in specific areas?

350. Organizational Applicability?

351. Which logical relationship does the PDM use most often?

352. How do you handle petty cash?

353. What are constraints that you might find during the Human Resource Planning process?

354. What is the Work Plan Standard?

355. Why do you do that?

356. Time for overtime?

357. Are there unresolved issues that need to be addressed?

358. When does monitoring begin?

359. Anything else?

2.16 Resource Breakdown Structure: Request For Information

360. What is the difference between % Complete and % work?

361. Changes based on input from stakeholders?

362. How difficult will it be to do specific activities on this Request For Information project?

363. Is predictive resource analysis being done?

364. Who is allowed to perform which functions?

365. When do they need the information?

366. How can this help you with team building?

367. Who is allowed to see what data about which resources?

368. Why do you do it?

369. What defines a successful Request For Information project?

370. How should the information be delivered?

371. What are the requirements for resource data?

372. What defines a successful Request For Information project?

373. Goals for the Request For Information project. What is each stakeholders desired outcome for the Request For Information project?

2.17 Activity Duration Estimates: Request For Information

374. How can others help Request For Information project managers understand your organizational context for Request For Information projects?

375. Which is correct?

376. Is risk identification completed regularly throughout the Request For Information project?

377. Does the case present a realistic scenario?

378. What are the Request For Information project management deliverables of each process group?

379. How difficult will it be to do specific activities on this Request For Information project?

380. How could you use each technique in your organization?

381. Who will provide training for the new application?

382. Why should Request For Information project managers strive to make jobs look easy?

383. What do you think about the WBSs for them?

384. Are procedures followed to ensure information is available to stakeholders in a timely manner?

385. How is the Request For Information project doing?

386. What are two suggestions for ensuring adequate change control on Request For Information projects that involve outside contracts?

387. What functions does this software provide that cannot be done easily using other tools such as a spreadsheet or database?

388. What is earned value?

389. What Request For Information project was the first to use modern Request For Information project management?

390. What is the shortest possible time it will take to complete this Request For Information project?

391. Are time, scope, cost, and quality monitored throughout the Request For Information project?

392. How does poking fun at technical professionals communications skills impact the industry and educational programs?

2.18 Duration Estimating Worksheet: Request For Information

393. Does the Request For Information project provide innovative ways for stakeholders to overcome obstacles or deliver better outcomes?

394. When do the individual activities need to start and finish?

395. For other activities, how much delay can be tolerated?

396. Small or large Request For Information project?

397. When does your organization expect to be able to complete it?

398. How should ongoing costs be monitored to try to keep the Request For Information project within budget?

399. How can the Request For Information project be displayed graphically to better visualize the activities?

400. Why estimate costs?

401. When, then?

402. What is an Average Request For Information project?

403. Can the Request For Information project be

constructed as planned?

404. What work will be included in the Request For Information project?

405. Is a construction detail attached (to aid in explanation)?

406. What utility impacts are there?

407. Why estimate time and cost?

408. Value pocket identification & quantification what are value pockets?

409. Is this operation cost effective?

410. Define the work as completely as possible. What work will be included in the Request For Information project?

2.19 Project Schedule: Request For Information

411. How effectively were issues able to be resolved without impacting the Request For Information project Schedule or Budget?

412. Why do you need schedules?

413. How can you minimize or control changes to Request For Information project schedules?

414. What documents, if any, will the subcontractor provide (eg Request For Information project schedule, quality plan etc)?

415. What is Request For Information project management?

416. How does a Request For Information project get to be a year late ?

417. Was the Request For Information project schedule reviewed by all stakeholders and formally accepted?

418. Are activities connected because logic dictates the order in which others occur?

419. Should you have a test for each code module?

420. Master Request For Information project schedule?

421. Why do you think schedule issues often cause the most conflicts on Request For Information projects?

422. What is the difference?

423. Is the Request For Information project schedule available for all Request For Information project team members to review?

424. Why is software Request For Information project disaster so common?

425. Schedule/cost recovery?

426. Are you working on the right risks?

427. Is infrastructure setup part of your Request For Information project?

428. What is the purpose of a Request For Information project schedule?

429. What is risk management?

2.20 Cost Management Plan: Request For Information

430. Vac -variance at completion, how much over/under budget do you expect to be?

431. Are status reports received per the Request For Information project Plan?

432. Have all team members been part of identifying risks?

433. Are meeting objectives identified for each meeting?

434. Designated small business reserve?

435. What will be the split of responsibilities of progress measurement and controls among the owner, contractor, subcontractors, and vendors?

436. Were Request For Information project team members involved in the development of activity & task decomposition?

437. Has a sponsor been identified?

438. If you sold 10x widgets on a day, what would the affect on costs be?

439. What would the life cycle costs be?

440. What does this mean to a cost or scheduler

manager?

441. Are changes in scope (deliverable commitments) agreed to by all affected groups & individuals?

442. Are all vendor contracts closed out?

443. Who should write the PEP?

444. What would you do differently what did not work?

445. Are Request For Information project team members committed fulltime?

446. Does the Request For Information project have a Statement of Work?

447. Have adequate resources been provided by management to ensure Request For Information project success?

448. Is Request For Information project status reviewed with the steering and executive teams at appropriate intervals?

2.21 Activity Cost Estimates: Request For Information

449. How do you manage cost?

450. Based on your Request For Information project communication management plan, what worked well?

451. Would you hire them again?

452. If you are asked to lower your estimate because the price is too high, what are your options?

453. How Award?

454. What is the estimators estimating history?

455. Are data needed on characteristics of care?

456. What is procurement?

457. Is there anything unique in this Request For Information projects scope statement that will affect resources?

458. How quickly can the task be done with the skills available?

459. What is included in indirect cost being allocated?

460. What are you looking for?

461. What were things that you did well, and could improve, and how?

462. Which contract type places the most risk on the seller?

463. How do you change activities?

464. What are the audit requirements?

465. Does the estimator have experience?

466. Who determines when the contractor is paid?

2.22 Cost Estimating Worksheet: Request For Information

467. What happens to any remaining funds not used?

468. Identify the timeframe necessary to monitor progress and collect data to determine how the selected measure has changed?

469. Will the Request For Information project collaborate with the local community and leverage resources?

470. How will the results be shared and to whom?

471. Is it feasible to establish a control group arrangement?

472. Is the Request For Information project responsive to community need?

473. What costs are to be estimated?

474. What can be included?

475. What will others want?

476. Ask: are others positioned to know, are others credible, and will others cooperate?

477. Does the Request For Information project provide innovative ways for stakeholders to overcome obstacles or deliver better outcomes?

478. Can a trend be established from historical performance data on the selected measure and are the criteria for using trend analysis or forecasting methods met?

479. What is the estimated labor cost today based upon this information?

480. What info is needed?

481. Who is best positioned to know and assist in identifying corresponding factors?

482. What additional Request For Information project(s) could be initiated as a result of this Request For Information project?

483. What is the purpose of estimating?

2.23 Cost Baseline: Request For Information

484. What do you want to measure ?

485. Have all approved changes to the schedule baseline been identified and impact on the Request For Information project documented?

486. Should a more thorough impact analysis be conducted?

487. Is the requested change request a result of changes in other Request For Information project(s)?

488. Review your risk triggers -have your risks changed?

489. Are there contingencies or conditions related to the acceptance?

490. Pcs for your new business. what would the life cycle costs be?

491. Verify business objectives. Are others appropriate, and well-articulated?

492. Does the suggested change request seem to represent a necessary enhancement to the product?

493. Has training and knowledge transfer of the operations organization been completed?

494. What is the reality?

495. Will the Request For Information project fail if the change request is not executed?

496. What is the consequence?

497. Request For Information project goals -should others be reconsidered?

498. How likely is it to go wrong?

499. What deliverables come first?

2.24 Quality Management Plan: Request For Information

500. How are senior leaders, employees, and your organization involved in supporting the community?

501. How does your organization perform analyzes to assess overall organizational performance and set priorities?

502. Documented results available?

503. How do senior leaders create and communicate values and performance expectations?

504. Were the right locations/samples tested for the right parameters?

505. Have you eliminated all duplicative tasks or manual efforts, where appropriate?

506. What are your organizations current levels and trends for the already stated measures related to customer satisfaction/ dissatisfaction and product/ service performance?

507. How will you know that a change is actually an improvement?

508. Who is responsible?

509. How are corresponding standards measured?

510. What methods are used?

511. No superfluous information or marketing narrative?

512. Who is approving the QAPP?

513. Have Request For Information project management standards and procedures been established and documented?

514. Who is responsible for writing the qapp?

515. What other teams / processes would be impacted by changes to the current process, and how?

516. What is your organizations strategic planning process?

517. How does training support what is important to your organization and the individual?

518. Who gets results of work?

519. Methodology followed?

2.25 Quality Metrics: Request For Information

520. Which data do others need in one place to target areas of improvement?

521. Was the overall quality better or worse than previous products?

522. Where is quality now?

523. What does this tell us?

524. Are interface issues coordinated?

525. What makes a visualization memorable?

526. Is material complete (and does it meet the standards)?

527. What can manufacturing professionals do to ensure quality is seen as an integral part of the entire product lifecycle?

528. Is quality culture a competitive advantage?

529. Does risk analysis documentation meet standards?

530. Did evaluation start on time?

531. How are requirements conflicts resolved?

532. Are there any open risk issues?

533. Are quality metrics defined?

534. How do you communicate results and findings to upper management?

535. There are many reasons to shore up quality-related metrics, and what metrics are important?

536. Do you know how much profit a 10% decrease in waste would generate?

537. Subjective quality component: customer satisfaction, how do you measure it?

538. Is the reporting frequency appropriate?

539. What percentage are outcome-based?

2.26 Process Improvement Plan: Request For Information

540. Management commitment at all levels?

541. Are you making progress on the improvement framework?

542. Purpose of goal: the motive is determined by asking, why do you want to achieve this goal?

543. Does your process ensure quality?

544. Why quality management?

545. What personnel are the sponsors for that initiative?

546. Are you meeting the quality standards?

547. Where do you focus?

548. What is the test-cycle concept?

549. The motive is determined by asking, Why do you want to achieve this goal?

550. Have the frequency of collection and the points in the process where measurements will be made been determined?

551. Has a process guide to collect the data been developed?

552. Are you following the quality standards?

553. If a process improvement framework is being used, which elements will help the problems and goals listed?

554. What personnel are the champions for the initiative?

555. Are you making progress on the goals?

556. What makes people good SPI coaches?

557. Modeling current processes is great, and will you ever see a return on that investment?

558. To elicit goal statements, do you ask a question such as, What do you want to achieve?

559. Where are you now?

2.27 Responsibility Assignment Matrix: Request For Information

560. How do you manage human resources?

561. The already stated responsible for the establishment of budgets and assignment of resources for overhead performance?

562. Performance to date and material commitment?

563. No rs: if a task has no one listed as responsible, who is getting the job done?

564. Is accountability placed at the lowest-possible level within the Request For Information project so that decisions can be made at that level?

565. Is cost and schedule performance measurement done in a consistent, systematic manner?

566. Do managers and team members provide helpful suggestions during review meetings?

567. Will too many Communicating responsibilities tangle the Request For Information project in unnecessary communications?

568. Availability – will the group or the person be available within the necessary time interval?

569. What do you need to implement earned value management?

570. Competencies and craftsmanship – what competencies are necessary and what level?

571. Are your organizations and items of cost assigned to each pool identified?

572. Does each activity-deliverable have exactly one Accountable responsibility, so that accountability is clear and decisions can be made quickly?

573. Ideas for developing soft skills at your organization?

574. Who is the Request For Information project Manager?

575. Are management actions taken to reduce indirect costs when there are significant adverse variances?

576. What are the assigned resources?

2.28 Roles and Responsibilities: Request For Information

577. What expectations were met?

578. What expectations were NOT met?

579. Concern: where are you limited or have no authority, where you can not influence?

580. Are your budgets supportive of a culture of quality data?

581. What should you do now to prepare yourself for a promotion, increased responsibilities or a different job?

582. Implementation of actions: Who are the responsible units?

583. Do the values and practices inherent in the culture of your organization foster or hinder the process?

584. What areas would you highlight for changes or improvements?

585. Is feedback clearly communicated and non-judgmental?

586. Key conclusions and recommendations: Are conclusions and recommendations relevant and acceptable?

587. Where are you most strong as a supervisor?

588. Are governance roles and responsibilities documented?

589. What should you do now to prepare for your career 5+ years from now?

590. Are Request For Information project team roles and responsibilities identified and documented?

591. Once the responsibilities are defined for the Request For Information project, have the deliverables, roles and responsibilities been clearly communicated to every participant?

592. Required skills, knowledge, experience?

593. Once the responsibilities are defined for the Request For Information project, have the deliverables, roles and responsibilities been clearly communicated to every participant?

594. What are your major roles and responsibilities in the area of performance measurement and assessment?

595. Are the quality assurance functions and related roles and responsibilities clearly defined?

596. Is there a training program in place for stakeholders covering expectations, roles and responsibilities and any addition knowledge others need to be good stakeholders?

2.29 Human Resource Management Plan: Request For Information

597. Are there dependencies with other initiatives or Request For Information projects?

598. Has the Request For Information project scope been baselined?

599. Are parking lot items captured?

600. Are change requests logged and managed?

601. Is there a Quality Management Plan?

602. Is there a Steering Committee in place?

603. Has a capability assessment been conducted?

604. Is there a set of procedures defining the scope, procedures, and deliverables defining quality control?

605. How are superior performers differentiated from average performers?

606. Quality of people required to meet the forecast needs of the department?

607. Is it standard practice to formally commit stakeholders to the Request For Information project via agreements?

608. Is the current culture aligned with the vision,

mission, and values of the department?

609. Are cause and effect determined for risks when others occur?

610. List the assumptions made to date. What did you have to assume to be true to complete the charter?

611. Are quality inspections and review activities listed in the Request For Information project schedule(s)?

612. Are multiple estimation methods being employed?

613. What were things that you need to improve?

2.30 Communications Management Plan: Request For Information

614. What to learn?

615. Who have you worked with in past, similar initiatives?

616. Do you have members of your team responsible for certain stakeholders?

617. In your work, how much time is spent on stakeholder identification?

618. Why do you manage communications?

619. Do you feel more overwhelmed by stakeholders?

620. What is Request For Information project communications management?

621. Who will use or be affected by the result of a Request For Information project?

622. Where do team members get information?

623. Why is stakeholder engagement important?

624. Which stakeholders can influence others?

625. Who to share with?

626. Do you prepare stakeholder engagement plans?

627. How much time does it take to do it?

628. Conflict resolution -which method when?

629. Who is the stakeholder?

630. What does the stakeholder need from the team?

631. Are there too many who have an interest in some aspect of your work?

632. What is the political influence?

633. Do you ask; can you recommend others for you to talk with about this initiative?

2.31 Risk Management Plan: Request For Information

634. What will the damage be?

635. What will drive change?

636. User involvement: do you have the right users?

637. Are there alternative opinions/solutions/processes you should explore?

638. Minimize cost and financial risk?

639. What are it-specific requirements?

640. What are the chances the risk event will occur?

641. Are the best people available?

642. Do end-users have realistic expectations?

643. What things are likely to change?

644. Is the number of people on the Request For Information project team adequate to do the job?

645. If you can not fix it, how do you do it differently?

646. Where do risks appear in the business phases?

647. Is the process supported by tools?

648. How would you suggest monitoring for risk transition indicators?

649. Do you have a consistent repeatable process that is actually used?

650. Was an original risk assessment/risk management plan completed?

651. How is risk monitoring performed?

652. What is the likelihood that your organization would accept responsibility for the risk?

653. How much risk can you tolerate?

2.32 Risk Register: Request For Information

654. Are implemented controls working as others should?

655. What evidence do you have to justify the likelihood score of the risk (audit, incident report, claim, complaints, inspection, internal review)?

656. What is a Community Risk Register?

657. Are there any gaps in the evidence?

658. Preventative actions - planned actions to reduce the likelihood a risk will occur and/or reduce the seriousness should it occur. What should you do now?

659. What are the major risks facing the Request For Information project?

660. Risk categories: what are the main categories of risks that should be addressed on this Request For Information project?

661. Recovery actions - planned actions taken once a risk has occurred to allow you to move on. What should you do after?

662. Budget and schedule: what are the estimated costs and schedules for performing risk-related activities?

663. What should the audit role be in establishing a risk management process?

664. What has changed since the last period?

665. What is the appropriate level of risk management for this Request For Information project?

666. What is a Risk?

667. When is it going to be done?

668. Schedule impact/severity estimated range (workdays) assume the event happens, what is the potential impact?

669. How could corresponding Risk affect the Request For Information project in terms of cost and schedule?

670. Technology risk -is the Request For Information project technically feasible?

671. Have other controls and solutions been implemented in other services which could be applied as an alternative to additional funding?

2.33 Probability and Impact Assessment: Request For Information

672. Are enough people available?

673. Can the Request For Information project proceed without assuming the risk?

674. What will be the likely political situation during the life of the Request For Information project?

675. Risks should be identified during which phase of Request For Information project management life cycle?

676. Does the software interface with new or unproven hardware or unproven vendor products?

677. What is the Request For Information project managers level of commitment and professionalism?

678. How much is the probability of a risk occurring?

679. Are flexibility and reuse paramount?

680. How realistic is the timing of introduction?

681. Do you use any methods to analyze risks?

682. What would be the effect of slippage?

683. Do you train all developers in the process?

684. Do you have specific methods that you use for each phase of the process?

685. Are testing tools available and suitable?

686. What risks are necessary to achieve success?

687. What significant shift will occur in governmental policies, laws, and regulations pertaining to specific industries?

688. What risks does the employee encounter?

689. What are the likely future requirements?

690. Are end-users enthusiastically committed to the Request For Information project and the system/product to be built?

2.34 Probability and Impact Matrix: Request For Information

691. Is the customer willing to participate in reviews?

692. What is the likelihood?

693. What are its business ethics?

694. Management -what contingency plans do you have if the risk becomes a reality?

695. Is there any sign of biased ranking?

696. What do you expect?

697. Are there new risks that mitigation strategies might introduce?

698. Are staff committed for the duration of the Request For Information project?

699. What is the industrial relations prevailing in this organization?

700. Is the present organizational structure for handling the Request For Information project sufficient?

701. What needs to be DONE?

702. How are you working with risks?

703. What are the channels available for distribution to the customer?

704. Amount of reused software?

705. Do you need a risk management plan?

706. Will there be an increase in the political conservatism?

707. Degree of confidence in estimated size estimate?

708. How can you understand and diagnose risks and identify sources?

2.35 Risk Data Sheet: Request For Information

709. What can you do?

710. How reliable is the data source?

711. What is the environment within which you operate (social trends, economic, community values, broad based participation, national directions etc.)?

712. What is the likelihood of it happening?

713. Whom do you serve (customers)?

714. What are the main opportunities available to you that you should grab while you can?

715. Has the most cost-effective solution been chosen?

716. What were the Causes that contributed?

717. Type of risk identified?

718. What are the main threats to your existence?

719. What are you trying to achieve (Objectives)?

720. What are your core values?

721. Potential for recurrence?

722. What are you here for (Mission)?

723. What actions can be taken to eliminate or remove risk?

724. What can happen?

725. Is the data sufficiently specified in terms of the type of failure being analyzed, and its frequency or probability?

726. During work activities could hazards exist?

2.36 Procurement Management Plan: Request For Information

727. Are milestone deliverables effectively tracked and compared to Request For Information project plan?

728. Is Request For Information project work proceeding in accordance with the original Request For Information project schedule?

729. Do Request For Information project managers participating in the Request For Information project know the Request For Information projects true status first hand?

730. What communication items need improvement?

731. Has the budget been baselined?

732. Are risk oriented checklists used during risk identification?

733. Is there an onboarding process in place?

734. Is an industry recognized mechanized support tool(s) being used for Request For Information project scheduling & tracking?

735. In which phase of the Acquisition Process Cycle does source qualifications reside?

736. Is there a procurement management plan in

place?

737. Do Request For Information project teams & team members report on status / activities / progress?

738. Are metrics used to evaluate and manage Vendors?

739. Are Request For Information project team members involved in detailed estimating and scheduling?

740. Are the Request For Information project plans updated on a frequent basis?

741. Is documentation created for communication with the suppliers and Vendors?

742. What are your quality assurance overheads?

743. Public engagement – did you get it right?

2.37 Source Selection Criteria: Request For Information

744. How can business terms and conditions be improved to yield more effective price competition?

745. Team leads: what is your process for assigning ratings?

746. What information is to be provided and when should it be provided?

747. What are the most common types of rating systems?

748. What are the limitations on pre-competitive range communications?

749. In the technical/management area, what criteria do you use to determine the final evaluation ratings?

750. Have team members been adequately trained?

751. What source selection software is your team using?

752. Is a letter of commitment from each proposed team member and key subcontractor included?

753. Is this a cost contract?

754. Who must be notified?

755. What does a sample rating scale look like?

756. What should be considered when developing evaluation standards?

757. Do proposed hours support content and schedule?

758. What aspects should the contracting officer brief the Request For Information project on prior to evaluation of proposals?

759. What common questions or problems are associated with debriefings?

760. What can not be disclosed?

761. Has all proposal data been loaded?

762. What documentation should be used to support the selection decision?

763. When and what information can be considered with offerors regarding past performance?

2.38 Stakeholder Management Plan: Request For Information

764. Are formal code reviews conducted?

765. Are all payments made according to the contract(s)?

766. Does the Request For Information project have a Quality Culture?

767. Where to get additional help?

768. Does the Request For Information project have a formal Request For Information project Charter?

769. Where will verification occur, and by whom?

770. When would you develop a Request For Information project Business Plan?

771. What is meant by activity dependencies and how do they relate to network diagramming?

772. Who is responsible for the post implementation review process?

773. What has to be purchased?

774. Do you use diagrams and tables to account for complex concepts and increase overall readability?

775. Has the scope management document been

updated and distributed to help prevent scope creep?

776. Does the Request For Information project have a Statement of Work?

777. Is the quality assurance team identified?

778. What are the advantages and disadvantages of using external contracted resources?

2.39 Change Management Plan: Request For Information

779. How prevalent is Resistance to Change?

780. Where do you want to be?

781. What does a resilient organization look like?

782. When developing your communication plan do you address : When should the given message be communicated?

783. What provokes organizational change?

784. What roles within your organization are affected, and how?

785. What did the people around you say about it?

786. Why would a Request For Information project run more smoothly when change management is emphasized from the beginning?

787. Have the business unit contacts been selected and notified?

788. Have the systems been configured and tested?

789. What risks may occur upfront, during implementation and after implementation?

790. Are there any restrictions on who can receive the

communications?

791. Is there a software application relevant to this deliverable?

792. What relationships will change?

793. How will you deal with anger about the restricting of communications due to confidentiality considerations?

794. When does it make sense to customize?

795. Who in the business it includes?

796. Has the target training audience been identified and nominated?

797. Do you need new systems?

798. Who will fund the training?

3.0 Executing Process Group: Request For Information

799. When do you share the scorecard with managers?

800. Are decisions made in a timely manner?

801. What areas were overlooked on this Request For Information project?

802. Do the partners have sufficient financial capacity to keep up the benefits produced by the programme?

803. Do the products created live up to the necessary quality?

804. Is the program supported by national and/or local organizations?

805. Who are the Request For Information project stakeholders?

806. Are escalated issues resolved promptly?

807. Could a new application negatively affect the current IT infrastructure?

808. What are the challenges Request For Information project teams face?

809. How will you know you did it?

810. Just how important is your work to the overall success of the Request For Information project?

811. Is activity definition the first process involved in Request For Information project time management?

812. After how many days will the lease cost be the same as the purchase cost for the equipment?

813. Who will be the main sponsor?

814. How well did the chosen processes fit the needs of the Request For Information project?

815. Does the Request For Information project team have the right skills?

816. What are deliverables of your Request For Information project?

3.1 Team Member Status Report: Request For Information

817. Why is it to be done?

818. Does the product, good, or service already exist within your organization?

819. How will resource planning be done?

820. How can you make it practical?

821. Are the attitudes of staff regarding Request For Information project work improving?

822. Does your organization have the means (staff, money, contract, etc.) to produce or to acquire the product, good, or service?

823. Will the staff do training or is that done by a third party?

824. Are your organizations Request For Information projects more successful over time?

825. Are the products of your organizations Request For Information projects meeting customers objectives?

826. When a teams productivity and success depend on collaboration and the efficient flow of information, what generally fails them?

827. The problem with Reward & Recognition Programs is that the truly deserving people all too often get left out. How can you make it practical?

828. How does this product, good, or service meet the needs of the Request For Information project and your organization as a whole?

829. Does every department have to have a Request For Information project Manager on staff?

830. Do you have an Enterprise Request For Information project Management Office (EPMO)?

831. What specific interest groups do you have in place?

832. What is to be done?

833. How much risk is involved?

834. Is there evidence that staff is taking a more professional approach toward management of your organizations Request For Information projects?

835. How it is to be done?

3.2 Change Request: Request For Information

836. Are you implementing itil processes?

837. What are the requirements for urgent changes?

838. What kind of information about the change request needs to be captured?

839. How many lines of code must be changed to implement the change?

840. What has an inspector to inspect and to check?

841. Why do you want to have a change control system?

842. How does a team identify the discrete elements of a configuration?

843. Who is included in the change control team?

844. Will this change conflict with other requirements changes (e.g., lead to conflicting operational scenarios)?

845. Who is communicating the change?

846. Have scm procedures for noting the change, recording it, and reporting it been followed?

847. How is quality being addressed on the Request

For Information project?

848. Describe how modifications, enhancements, defects and/or deficiencies shall be notified (e.g. Problem Reports, Change Requests etc) and managed. Detail warranty and/or maintenance periods?

849. What should be regulated in a change control operating instruction?

850. How can you ensure that changes have been made properly?

851. Will new change requests be acknowledged in a timely manner?

852. Which requirements attributes affect the risk to reliability the most?

853. What is the change request log?

854. How shall the implementation of changes be recorded?

3.3 Change Log: Request For Information

855. Where do changes come from?

856. How does this change affect scope?

857. Is the submitted change a new change or a modification of a previously approved change?

858. When was the request submitted?

859. Is the change request open, closed or pending?

860. Is the requested change request a result of changes in other Request For Information project(s)?

861. Do the described changes impact on the integrity or security of the system?

862. How does this relate to the standards developed for specific business processes?

863. Is the change backward compatible without limitations?

864. When was the request approved?

865. Is this a mandatory replacement?

866. Will the Request For Information project fail if the change request is not executed?

867. How does this change affect the timeline of the schedule?

868. Who initiated the change request?

869. Does the suggested change request represent a desired enhancement to the products functionality?

870. Is the change request within Request For Information project scope?

3.4 Decision Log: Request For Information

871. Linked to original objective?

872. What alternatives/risks were considered?

873. Behaviors; what are guidelines that the team has identified that will assist them with getting the most out of team meetings?

874. With whom was the decision shared or considered?

875. What is the line where eDiscovery ends and document review begins?

876. What is the average size of your matters in an applicable measurement?

877. At what point in time does loss become unacceptable?

878. How do you know when you are achieving it?

879. Do strategies and tactics aimed at less than full control reduce the costs of management or simply shift the cost burden?

880. What are the cost implications?

881. Who will be given a copy of this document and where will it be kept?

882. It becomes critical to track and periodically revisit both operational effectiveness; Are you noticing all that you need to, and are you interpreting what you see effectively?

883. Meeting purpose; why does this team meet?

884. How effective is maintaining the log at facilitating organizational learning?

885. Is everything working as expected?

886. Is your opponent open to a non-traditional workflow, or will it likely challenge anything you do?

887. What was the rationale for the decision?

888. How does provision of information, both in terms of content and presentation, influence acceptance of alternative strategies?

889. What makes you different or better than others companies selling the same thing?

890. How does an increasing emphasis on cost containment influence the strategies and tactics used?

3.5 Quality Audit: Request For Information

891. Do all staff have the necessary authority and resources to deliver what is expected of them?

892. Are training programs documented?

893. Do the acceptance procedures and specifications include the criteria for acceptance/rejection, define the process to be used, and specify the measuring and test equipment that is to be used?

894. How do you know what, specifically, is required of you in your work?

895. How does your organization know that the range and quality of its accommodation, catering and transportation services are appropriately effective and constructive?

896. Are there sufficient personnel having the necessary education, background, training, and experience to assure that all operations are correctly performed?

897. How does the organization know that its system for maintaining and advancing the capabilities of its staff, particularly in relation to the Mission of the organization, is appropriately effective and constructive?

898. Is refuse and garbage adequately stored and

disposed of with sufficient frequency to prevent contamination?

899. How does your organization ensure that equipment is appropriately maintained and producing valid results?

900. What are you trying to accomplish with this audit?

901. How does your organization know that its policy management system is appropriately effective and constructive?

902. How does your organization know that its Mission, Vision and Values Statements are appropriate and effectively guiding your organization?

903. Is the continuing professional education of key personnel account fored in detail?

904. How does your organization know that its research funding systems are appropriately effective and constructive in enabling quality research outcomes?

905. Are measuring and test equipment that have been placed out of service suitably identified and excluded from use in any device reconditioning operation?

906. How does your organization know that its system for commercializing research outputs is appropriately effective and constructive?

907. How does your organization know that its system

for attending to the health and wellbeing of its staff is appropriately effective and constructive?

908. Is quality audit a prerequisite for program accreditation or program recognition?

909. How does your organization know that its system for inducting new staff to maximize workplace contributions are appropriately effective and constructive?

910. Does the audit organization have experience in performing the required work for entities of your type and size?

3.6 Team Directory: Request For Information

911. How and in what format should information be presented?

912. Who are your stakeholders (customers, sponsors, end users, team members)?

913. Who will be the stakeholders on your next Request For Information project?

914. How will you accomplish and manage the objectives?

915. Process decisions: are there any statutory or regulatory issues relevant to the timely execution of work?

916. What needs to be communicated?

917. Who are the Team Members?

918. Who will write the meeting minutes and distribute?

919. Why is the work necessary?

920. Where will the product be used and/or delivered or built when appropriate?

921. Process decisions: do invoice amounts match accepted work in place?

922. Have you decided when to celebrate the Request For Information projects completion date?

923. Process decisions: do job conditions warrant additional actions to collect job information and document on-site activity?

924. Timing: when do the effects of communication take place?

925. When will you produce deliverables?

926. Contract requirements complied with?

927. Process decisions: which organizational elements and which individuals will be assigned management functions?

928. Where should the information be distributed?

3.7 Team Operating Agreement: Request For Information

929. Resource allocation: how will individual team members account for time and expenses, and how will this be allocated in the team budget?

930. What resources can be provided for the team in terms of equipment, space, time for training, protected time and space for meetings, and travel allowances?

931. The method to be used in the decision making process; Will it be consensus, majority rule, or the supervisor having the final say?

932. Do you vary your voice pace, tone and pitch to engage participants and gain involvement?

933. Do you brief absent members after they view meeting notes or listen to a recording?

934. What is culture?

935. Are team roles clearly defined and accepted?

936. What are some potential sources of conflict among team members?

937. Is compensation based on team and individual performance?

938. What are the safety issues/risks that need to be

addressed and/or that the team needs to consider?

939. Do you solicit member feedback about meetings and what would make them better?

940. Do you call or email participants to ensure understanding, follow-through and commitment to the meeting outcomes?

941. Do you ensure that all participants know how to use the required technology?

942. To whom do you deliver your services?

943. Reimbursements: how will the team members be reimbursed for expenses and time commitments?

944. Do you determine the meeting length and time of day?

945. What administrative supports will be put in place to support the team and the teams supervisor?

946. Do you prevent individuals from dominating the meeting?

947. Does your team need access to all documents and information at all times?

948. How will your group handle planned absences?

3.8 Team Performance Assessment: Request For Information

949. What are you doing specifically to develop the leaders around you?

950. When a reviewer complains about method variance, what is the essence of the complaint?

951. To what degree does the teams approach to its work allow for modification and improvement over time?

952. Effects of crew composition on crew performance: Does the whole equal the sum of its parts?

953. Social categorization and intergroup behaviour: Does minimal intergroup discrimination make social identity more positive?

954. To what degree does the teams purpose constitute a broader, deeper aspiration than just accomplishing short-term goals?

955. To what degree will team members, individually and collectively, commit time to help themselves and others learn and develop skills?

956. If you are worried about method variance before you collect data, what sort of design elements might you include to reduce or eliminate the threat of method variance?

957. To what degree can the team measure progress against specific goals?

958. To what degree are the skill areas critical to team performance present?

959. To what degree are fresh input and perspectives systematically caught and added (for example, through information and analysis, new members, and senior sponsors)?

960. To what degree does the teams work approach provide opportunity for members to engage in fact-based problem solving?

961. To what degree do all members feel responsible for all agreed-upon measures?

962. To what degree do team members articulate the teams work approach?

963. To what degree can team members vigorously define the teams purpose in considerations with others who are not part of the functioning team?

964. To what degree do team members frequently explore the teams purpose and its implications?

965. To what degree do team members agree with the goals, relative importance, and the ways in which achievement will be measured?

966. What structural changes have you made or are you preparing to make?

967. Delaying market entry: how long is too long?

968. To what degree are the members clear on what they are individually responsible for and what they are jointly responsible for?

3.9 Team Member Performance Assessment: Request For Information

969. Which training platform formats (i.e., mobile, virtual, videogame-based) were implemented in your effort(s)?

970. Does statute or regulation require the job responsibility?

971. What are they responsible for?

972. How do you currently account for your results in the teams achievement?

973. What entity leads the process, selects a potential restructuring option and develops the plan?

974. To what degree do team members feel that the purpose of the team is important, if not exciting?

975. To what degree does the team possess adequate membership to achieve its ends?

976. What evaluation results did you have?

977. How do you know that all team members are learning?

978. How are assessments designed, delivered, and otherwise used to maximize training?

979. Do the goals support your organizations goals?

980. Verify business objectives. Are they appropriate, and well-articulated?

981. What are best practices for delivering and developing training evaluations to maximize the benefits of leveraging emerging technologies?

982. How should adaptive assessments be implemented?

983. How accurately is your plan implemented?

984. What is needed for effective data teams?

985. What qualities does a successful Team leader possess?

986. What are best practices in use for the performance measurement system?

3.10 Issue Log: Request For Information

987. Who needs to know and how much?

988. Who is the issue assigned to?

989. Why do you manage human resources?

990. How were past initiatives successful?

991. What is the stakeholders political influence?

992. Are stakeholder roles recognized by your organization?

993. Who do you turn to if you have questions?

994. Is there an important stakeholder who is actively opposed and will not receive messages?

995. Is it a change in scope?

996. Which team member will work with each stakeholder?

997. What effort will a change need?

998. How do you manage communications?

999. What is the impact on the risks?

1000. Who reported the issue?

1001. Is the issue log kept in a safe place?

1002. What is the stakeholders level of authority?

4.0 Monitoring and Controlling Process Group: Request For Information

1003. Is there sufficient funding available for this?

1004. Use: how will they use the information?

1005. Were escalated issues resolved promptly?

1006. What areas does the group agree are the biggest success on the Request For Information project?

1007. What departments are involved in its daily operation?

1008. In what way has the program come up with innovative measures for problem-solving?

1009. How will staff learn how to use the deliverables?

1010. How many more potential communications channels were introduced by the discovery of the new stakeholders?

1011. Did the Request For Information project team have the right skills?

1012. Purpose: toward what end is the evaluation being conducted?

1013. How well did the chosen processes fit the needs

of the Request For Information project?

1014. Have operating capacities been created and/or reinforced in partners?

1015. Are the services being delivered?

1016. What is the timeline?

1017. Does the solution fit in with organizations technical architectural requirements?

1018. How many potential communications channels exist on the Request For Information project?

4.1 Project Performance Report: Request For Information

1019. What degree are the relative importance and priority of the goals clear to all team members?

1020. To what degree does the formal organization make use of individual resources and meet individual needs?

1021. Next Steps?

1022. To what degree will new and supplemental skills be introduced as the need is recognized?

1023. To what degree are the tasks requirements reflected in the flow and storage of information?

1024. To what degree is there centralized control of information sharing?

1025. What is the degree to which rules govern information exchange between individuals within your organization?

1026. To what degree will the team adopt a concrete, clearly understood, and agreed-upon approach that will result in achievement of the teams goals?

1027. To what degree does the teams work approach provide opportunity for members to engage in results-based evaluation?

1028. How will procurement be coordinated with other Request For Information project aspects, such as scheduling and performance reporting?

1029. To what degree are sub-teams possible or necessary?

1030. To what degree do individual skills and abilities match task demands?

1031. To what degree can team members meet frequently enough to accomplish the teams ends?

1032. To what degree is the information network consistent with the structure of the formal organization?

4.2 Variance Analysis: Request For Information

1033. Can the relationship with problem customers be restructured so that there is a win-win situation?

1034. Are there knowledgeable Request For Information projections of future performance?

1035. Does the scheduling system identify in a timely manner the status of work?

1036. What does an unfavorable overhead volume variance mean?

1037. Do work packages consist of discrete tasks which are adequately described?

1038. What is the total budget for the Request For Information project (including estimates for authorized and unpriced work)?

1039. What is the actual cost of work performed?

1040. Are indirect costs accumulated for comparison with the corresponding budgets?

1041. How do you manage changes in the nature of the overhead requirements?

1042. What is the incurrence of actual indirect costs in excess of budgets, by element of expense?

1043. Are material costs reported within the same period as that in which BCWP is earned for that material?

1044. What causes selling price variance?

1045. Are there changes in the overhead pool and/or organization structures?

1046. Are the requirements for all items of overhead established by rational, traceable processes?

1047. Are control accounts opened and closed based on the start and completion of work contained therein?

1048. Are the actual costs used for variance analysis reconcilable with data from the accounting system?

1049. When, during the last four quarters, did a primary business event occur causing a fluctuation?

1050. Is all contract work included in the CWBS?

1051. What should management do?

4.3 Earned Value Status: Request For Information

1052. If earned value management (EVM) is so good in determining the true status of a Request For Information project and Request For Information project its completion, why is it that hardly any one uses it in information systems related Request For Information projects?

1053. Earned value can be used in almost any Request For Information project situation and in almost any Request For Information project environment. it may be used on large Request For Information projects, medium sized Request For Information projects, tiny Request For Information projects (in cut-down form), complex and simple Request For Information projects and in any market sector. some people, of course, know all about earned value, they have used it for years - but perhaps not as effectively as they could have?

1054. Are you hitting your Request For Information projects targets?

1055. When is it going to finish?

1056. Validation is a process of ensuring that the developed system will actually achieve the stakeholders desired outcomes; Are you building the right product? What do you validate?

1057. How much is it going to cost by the finish?

1058. Verification is a process of ensuring that the developed system satisfies the stakeholders agreements and specifications; Are you building the product right? What do you verify?

1059. Where are your problem areas?

1060. Where is evidence-based earned value in your organization reported?

1061. What is the unit of forecast value?

1062. How does this compare with other Request For Information projects?

4.4 Risk Audit: Request For Information

1063. Does your board meet regularly and document all decisions and actions?

1064. Are some people working on multiple Request For Information projects?

1065. Does your organization have or has considered the need for insurance covers: public liability, professional indemnity and directors and officers liability?

1066. Are the software tools integrated with each other?

1067. Is safety information provided to all involved?

1068. Will an appropriate standard of care be applied to all involved?

1069. Will participants be required to sign a legally counselled waiver or risk disclaimer when entering an event?

1070. Have customers been involved fully in the definition of requirements?

1071. Can assurance be expanded beyond the traditional audit without undermining independence?

1072. Do you record and file all audits?

1073. Tradeoff: how much risk can be tolerated and still deliver the products where they need to be?

1074. Do you have a clear plan for the future that describes what you want to do and how you are going to do it?

1075. Number of users of the product?

1076. What impact does experience with one client have on decisions made for other clients during the risk-assessment process?

1077. How risk averse are you?

1078. Do your financial policies and procedures ensure that each step in financial handling (receipt, recording, banking, reporting) is not completed by one person?

1079. How do you govern assets?

1080. Do you have financial policies and procedures in place to guide officers of your organization/treasurer/ general members?

4.5 Contractor Status Report: Request For Information

1081. What process manages the contracts?

1082. What was the budget or estimated cost for your organizations services?

1083. Who can list a Request For Information project as organization experience, your organization or a previous employee of your organization?

1084. What was the final actual cost?

1085. What was the overall budget or estimated cost?

1086. What was the actual budget or estimated cost for your organizations services?

1087. How does the proposed individual meet each requirement?

1088. Describe how often regular updates are made to the proposed solution. Are corresponding regular updates included in the standard maintenance plan?

1089. What are the minimum and optimal bandwidth requirements for the proposed solution?

1090. How long have you been using the services?

1091. If applicable; describe your standard schedule for new software version releases. Are new software version releases included in the standard maintenance plan?

1092. How is risk transferred?

1093. What is the average response time for answering a support call?

1094. Are there contractual transfer concerns?

4.6 Formal Acceptance: Request For Information

1095. Was the Request For Information project goal achieved?

1096. Who supplies data?

1097. What are the requirements against which to test, Who will execute?

1098. What lessons were learned about your Request For Information project management methodology?

1099. What function(s) does it fill or meet?

1100. Does it do what Request For Information project team said it would?

1101. General estimate of the costs and times to complete the Request For Information project?

1102. How does your team plan to obtain formal acceptance on your Request For Information project?

1103. Who would use it?

1104. Is formal acceptance of the Request For Information project product documented and distributed?

1105. What features, practices, and processes proved to be strengths or weaknesses?

1106. Do you perform formal acceptance or burn-in tests?

1107. Was business value realized?

1108. What can you do better next time?

1109. Was the Request For Information project managed well?

1110. Was the Request For Information project work done on time, within budget, and according to specification?

1111. How well did the team follow the methodology?

1112. Was the client satisfied with the Request For Information project results?

1113. Do you buy pre-configured systems or build your own configuration?

1114. What is the Acceptance Management Process?

5.0 Closing Process Group: Request For Information

1115. What is the Request For Information project Management Process?

1116. What is the overall risk of the Request For Information project to your organization?

1117. Did the Request For Information project team have the right skills?

1118. How critical is the Request For Information project success to the success of your organization?

1119. Did the Request For Information project management methodology work?

1120. Were the outcomes different from the already stated planned?

1121. Was the schedule met?

1122. What is the amount of funding and what Request For Information project phases are funded?

1123. Did the delivered product meet the specified requirements and goals of the Request For Information project?

1124. Were risks identified and mitigated?

1125. What level of risk does the proposed budget

represent to the Request For Information project?

1126. Is the Request For Information project funded?

1127. Are there funding or time constraints?

1128. What could be done to improve the process?

1129. How dependent is the Request For Information project on other Request For Information projects or work efforts?

5.1 Procurement Audit: Request For Information

1130. Are risks in the external environment identified, for example: Budgetary constraints?

1131. Do established procedures ensure that computer programs will not pay the same group of invoices twice?

1132. Are trial balances taken weekly for general ledgers for all funds?

1133. Were any additional works or deliveries admissible without the need for a new procurement procedure?

1134. Which are main risks and controls of each phase?

1135. Are staff members evaluated in accordance with the terms of existing negotiated agreements?

1136. Are procedures established on how orders will be shipped?

1137. Are internal control systems in place?

1138. When you set social or environmental conditions for the performance of the contract, were corresponding compatible with the law and was adequate information given to the candidates?

1139. Is there a policy on making purchases locally where possible?

1140. Does the procurement function/unit have the ability to secure best performance from contractors?

1141. Where your organization engaged an expert, was the contract awarded in compliance with procurement regulations?

1142. Is the purchasing department consulted on favorable purchasing opportunities, economic ordering quantities, and revision of purchasing specifications?

1143. Is the issuance of purchase orders scheduled so that orders are not issued daily?

1144. Is the appropriate procurement approach being chosen (considering for example the possibility of contracting out work or procuring low value items through a specific low cost procuring system)?

1145. Is there a policy covering the relationship of other departments with vendors?

1146. Is there a formal program of inservice training for personnel in the business management function?

1147. Are there appropriate controls in place to ensure that the procurement Request For Information project complies with relevant legislation?

1148. Months to reflect any changes in policy?

1149. If a purchase order calls for a cost-plus

agreement, is the method of determining how final charges will be determined specified?

5.2 Contract Close-Out: Request For Information

1150. Parties: who is involved?

1151. Why Outsource?

1152. Change in knowledge?

1153. Have all acceptance criteria been met prior to final payment to contractors?

1154. Was the contract complete without requiring numerous changes and revisions?

1155. Has each contract been audited to verify acceptance and delivery?

1156. How is the contracting office notified of the automatic contract close-out?

1157. Have all contracts been closed?

1158. Parties: Authorized?

1159. How/when used ?

1160. Have all contracts been completed?

1161. Change in attitude or behavior?

1162. Was the contract sufficiently clear so as not to result in numerous disputes and misunderstandings?

1163. What is capture management?

1164. How does it work?

1165. Are the signers the authorized officials?

1166. Change in circumstances?

1167. What happens to the recipient of services?

1168. Have all contract records been included in the Request For Information project archives?

1169. Was the contract type appropriate?

5.3 Project or Phase Close-Out: Request For Information

1170. What is a Risk Management Process?

1171. In addition to assessing whether the Request For Information project was successful, it is equally critical to analyze why it was or was not fully successful. Are you including this?

1172. What was the preferred delivery mechanism?

1173. What were the desired outcomes?

1174. Planned completion date?

1175. What were the actual outcomes?

1176. Were messages directly related to the release strategy or phases of the Request For Information project?

1177. What was expected from each stakeholder?

1178. Is the lesson based on actual Request For Information project experience rather than on independent research?

1179. What could have been improved?

1180. What information did each stakeholder need to contribute to the Request For Information projects success?

1181. What were the goals and objectives of the communications strategy for the Request For Information project?

1182. Did the Request For Information project management methodology work?

1183. Have business partners been involved extensively, and what data was required for them?

1184. What information is each stakeholder group interested in?

1185. If you were the Request For Information project sponsor, how would you determine which Request For Information project team(s) and/or individuals deserve recognition?

1186. What went well?

1187. What are the marketing communication needs for each stakeholder?

5.4 Lessons Learned: Request For Information

1188. How effective were Best Practices & Lessons Learned from prior Request For Information projects utilized in this Request For Information project?

1189. What is the impact of tax policy?

1190. What is the quality and content of communication?

1191. Recommendation: what do you recommend should be done to ensure that others throughout your organization can benefit from what you have learned?

1192. How useful was the format and content of the Request For Information project Status Report to you?

1193. What was the single greatest success and the single greatest shortcoming or challenge from the Request For Information projects perspective?

1194. What did you do right?

1195. What would you like to see better documented about how to use existing processes on this type of Request For Information project?

1196. How well did the Request For Information project Manager respond to questions or comments related to the Request For Information project?

1197. How effective was the acceptance management process?

1198. How adequately involved did you feel in Request For Information project decisions?

1199. How much time is required for the task?

1200. How well is the build process working?

1201. How mature are the observations?

1202. Was the Request For Information project significantly delayed/hampered by outside dependencies (outside to the Request For Information project, that is)?

1203. How effective were the communications materials in providing and orienting team members about the details of the Request For Information project?

1204. What needs to be done over or differently?

1205. What is below the surface?

Index

managed   7, 29, 62, 70, 72, 79, 86, 89, 96, 102, 195, 222, 254
management 1, 3-5, 8-9, 18, 20, 23, 29, 32, 38, 48, 64, 70-71, 73, 78, 80-81, 83-85, 113, 120, 124, 126, 130, 138-139, 141-143, 149-151, 155, 157-158, 171-172, 175-179, 185-186, 188-189, 191-192, 195, 197, 199-200, 202-203, 205-206, 209, 211, 213, 215, 218, 220, 225, 228, 231, 246-247, 253-255, 258, 261-263, 265
manager   7, 9, 16, 30, 35, 115, 131, 143, 149, 178, 192, 220, 264
managers   2, 129, 171, 191, 203, 209, 217
manages   83-84, 251
managing   2, 86, 129, 131, 134
mandatory   223
manner   24, 79, 131, 155, 171, 191, 217, 222, 245
mantle 106
manual   185
mapped   30
Mapping   62, 64-65
marked   149
market 22, 163, 236, 247
marketer   7
marketing   118, 146, 186, 263
Master 175
material   156, 164, 187, 191, 246
materials   1, 265
matrices   147
Matrix 2-5, 135, 147, 191, 205
matter 28, 56
matters   225
mature 265
maximize   229, 237-238
maximum   131
meaning   161
meaningful   57, 109, 155
measurable   36, 40
measure   2, 9, 20-21, 32, 35, 44, 47-50, 52, 54-55, 57, 67, 75-76, 80, 83, 88, 92, 95, 97, 100, 135, 158, 181-183, 188, 235
measured   23, 45-47, 49-50, 56-57, 82, 96, 101, 185, 235
measures   51, 53-54, 56, 58, 60, 66-67, 71, 76, 91, 94, 98, 185, 235, 241
measuring   97, 155-156, 227-228
mechanical   1
mechanism   151, 262
mechanized   209

Printed in Great Britain
by Amazon

66087911R00184